Lewis Leaming Forman

The Difference between the Genitive and Dative Used with

Epi to Denote Superpostion

Lewis Leaming Forman

The Difference between the Genitive and Dative Used with Epi to Denote Superpostion

ISBN/EAN: 9783337811471

Printed in Europe, USA, Canada, Australia, Japan

Cover: Foto ©Thomas Meinert / pixelio.de

More available books at **www.hansebooks.com**

THE DIFFERENCE

BETWEEN

THE GENITIVE AND DATIVE

USED WITH ἐπί TO

DENOTE SUPERPOSITION

BY

LEWIS LEAMING FORMAN, A. M.

A DISSERTATION ACCEPTED FOR THE DEGREE OF DOCTOR
OF PHILOSOPHY IN THE JOHNS HOPKINS
UNIVERSITY, FEBRUARY, 1894

———

BALTIMORE
1894

PRESS OF
THE FRIEDENWALD COMPANY
BALTIMORE

" Vix quidquam tam lubricum est in syntaxi linguarum, quam hi loci, qui sunt de praepositionibus et de coniunctionibus." These words of G. Hermann,[1] though written many years ago (1831), must be recognized, however regretfully, as still true by any one who has attempted to answer even some less important question in prepositional usage. Classification he finds difficult, at times impossible, and the opinions of authorities widely divergent.

On the general theory of prepositions, it is true, Delbrück announced in 1879 the following consensus of judgment : " Ueber die ursprüngliche Anwendung dieser Präpositionen (ἀνά, ἐπί, παρά, περί, πρός, πρό, ἐν, ἐκ, ξύν) ist man jetzt zu einer übereinstimmenden Meinung gelangt. Man nimmt allgemein an, dass die Präpositionen ursprünglich wie alle Wörter *Freiwörter* (sog. Adverbia) waren, und dann *Begleitwörter* wurden, und zwar von Anfang an in grösster Ausdehnung verbale Begleitwörter, dagegen Anfangs seltener und erst im Laufe der Zeit häufiger werdend nominale Begleitwörter. In der ältesten Zeit war es die wesentliche Aufgabe der Präpositionen, die Richtung der im Verbum ausgedrückten Handlung näher zu bestimmen, die Beziehung der Handlung aber auf einen Gegenstand drückte der Casus allein aus, ohne Beihülfe der Präpositionen."[2] So essentially say Kühner,[3] Curtius,[4] Whitney[5] and others before this date, and so Paul,[6] Brugmann,[7] Vogrinz[8] and others since. But it is only upon this general theory that a consensus can be obtained—so general indeed that it must ignore the question of the ultimate origin of

[1] Opuscula, vol. V, p. 50, quoted by Sobolewski, *De Praepositionum Usu Aristophaneo.*

[2] *Syntaktische Forschungen*, IV 126.

[3] *Grammatik der griech. Sprache* (1870), II, §428, 3 and 4.

[4] *Erläuterungen* (1875), p. 176.

[5] *Language and the Study of Lang.* (1877), p. 276.

[6] *Principien der Sprachgeschichte* (1886), p. 316.

[7] *Griechische Grammatik* (Müller's Handbuch, II, 1890), §195.

[8] *Grammatik des homerischen Dialektes* (1889), p. 206.

4

prepositions,[1] *i. e.* whether or not they contain the stems of *Begriffswörter;* whereas, if one enters into particulars even so slightly as to ask for a definition of the difference between the true and the "improper" preps., or what preps., if any, go with the true gen. case, he will obtain a great diversity of answers. Curtius, for instance, finds that the gen. depends upon ἀντί, πρό, διά, ὑπέρ "und vielen andern—gerade in der Weise wie von unserm Angesichts, laut, kraft."[2] Delbrück takes issue with him, though admitting the Curtius-construction as a probability for ἀντί and a possibility for διά, because they may belong to the class of "unechten, d. h. aus Nominalstämmen gebildeten Präpositionen."[3] Vogrinz, *Gram. des homerischen Dialektes,* takes the gen. to be adnominal with ἀντί (p. 211), διά (p. 214), κατά sometimes (p. 215), ὑπέρ (p. 216), παρά "schwer zu entscheiden" (p. 222), πρός "allem Anschein nach" (p. 223). Delbrück now says : " Der echte Genitiv findet sich bei ἀντί, ὑπέρ, διά, ἐπί, ποτί, ἀνά, ἀμφί, περί, μετά. Bei ἀντί, ὑπέρ und διά dürfte es der alte adnominale Genitiv sein, welcher uns bei den unechten Präp. begegnet."[4] It will be observed that as these lists are not co-extensive, the slipperiness of which Hermann complains is still present.

For the purposes of the present essay, however, these larger questions need not be taken up and the general theory as above presented may be subscribed to. We proceed therefore to the proper subject of the essay—the difference between the gen. and dat. used with ἐπί to express superposition, or, to take a concrete case,

What is the Attic Greek prose for 'with his hat on his head'? Is it ἐπὶ τῆς κεφαλῆς, or ἐπὶ τῇ κεφαλῇ? Or if either, is there any shade of difference in the meaning?

For the translation of so simple a phrase, one might expect

---

[1] See Grassmann, *Ursprung der Präpositionen,* Kuhn's *Zeitschrift,* XXIII (1877), p. 559. He maintains (p. 563) : " Keine ächte Präposition ist aus einem Begriffswort entsprungen," as also : " Keine ächte Präp. ist als Casus zu fassen." See on the contrary for παρά, Osthoff, *Morph. Unters.* IV 283, Anm., " der alte Instrumental," and for περί and ἐνί, Brugmann, *Gr. Gram.,* §194 (locat.). So too διά (διαί), πρό, and others have been reckoned among the preps. "in quibus terminatio alicuius nominis latet, ex quo genetivus pendeat," J. A. Heilmann, *De Genetivi Graeci maxima Homerici usu* (1873), p. 25, note 2,

[2] *Erläuterungen,* p. 177.

[3] *Synt. Forsch.* IV 134.

[4] *Vergleichende Syntax der indogermanischen Sprachen* (1893), p. 762.

clear rules and distinctions laid down even in the elementary books. The question is not one of origins. No matter what its derivation, affinities or ultimate meaning, ἐπί is certainly the proper preposition, while the case of the substantive should be settled by an examination of the remains of Greek literature; and, if both cases prove to be allowed, the difference between them, if worth anything, should appear at the same time. Only in this last matter need one feel drawn beyond the Greek in search of the Indo-Germanic basis of distinction.

Yet simple as the question seems, scholars are much at variance about it. Stated in general terms the question is:

1) Does Attic Greek prose employ ἐπί with both genitive and dative to express concrete superposition of one body upon another?

2) If so, what is the difference, if any, between the two forms of expression?

The answers of the following authorities I quote at some length, that their text may be at hand for reference.

1) Kühner, *Grammatik der griech. Sprache* (1870), II, §438: "ἐπί mit dem Dativ, 1) räumlich zur Angabe des Verweilens nicht nur, wie beim Gen., *auf*, sondern, und zwar häufiger, in erweiterter Bedeutung *an* od. *bei* einem Orte od. Gegenstande." He then quotes among other instances of *auf* Xen. An. VII 4, 4 οἱ Θρᾷκες τὰς ἀλωπεκίδας ἐπὶ ταῖς κεφαλαῖς φοροῦσι καὶ τοῖς ὠσὶ καὶ ζειρὰς (Oberkleider) μέχρι τῶν ποδῶν ἐπὶ τῶν ἵππων ἔχουσιν, remarking "ἐπί c. dat. rein räumlich, aber ἐπὶ τῶν ἵππων, insofern die Pferde als thätig gedacht werden; so Plat. Conv. 212e ἐπὶ τῇ κεφαλῇ ἔχων τὰς ταινίας, aber kurz vorher ταινίας ἔχων ἐπὶ τῆς κεφαλῆς."

2) Krüger, *Griechische Grammatik* (1875), §68, 41, 1: "Bei ἐπί mit dem Gen. wird eine mehr zufällige, freiere Verbindung gedacht; bei ἐπί mit dem Dat. schwebt mehr der Begriff der Zugehörigkeit vor."

3) Rutherford, *Babrius* (1883), p. 7: "The correct Attic usage is very simple, the best writers of prose and comedy limiting ἐπί c. gen. to position or motion upon an object or surface, and ἐπί c. dat. to position or motion at or near. Thus a floating body is ἐπὶ ποταμοῦ, a city ἐπὶ ποταμῷ. A wounded man may be carried home ἐπὶ θυρῶν, a beggar sits ἐπὶ θύραις. In tragedy this distinction is not observed, and ἐπί c. dat. is also used to convey the sense which prose writers confine to the genitive. In Thucydides the prose usage has not yet become absolute, and although several

6

deviations from the rule, such as ἀκάτιον ἐπὶ ἁμάξῃ κατακομίζειν (4, 67), admit of easy correction, yet the undoubted dat. in 2, 80 τοὺς ὁπλίτας ἐπὶ ναυσὶ πέμπουσι, 4, 10 ἐπὶ ταῖς ναυσὶ ῥᾳστοί εἰσιν ἀμύνεσθαι, proves that such emendation is as uncalled for in the immature Attic of Thucydides as it would be in Herod. or Xen. The Ionic and poetic laxity also crops up in the Symposium, where Plato allows himself a poet's license, and in the same paragraph (212e) are found the poetical ἐπὶ τῇ κεφαλῇ ἔχων τὰς ταινίας, and the prosaic ταινίας ἔχοντα ἐπὶ τῆς κεφαλῆς. In no writer, however, is the genuine prose signification of ἐπί c. dat. ever accredited to ἐπί c. gen.,[1] although the meaning 'in the direction of' sometimes brings ἐπί close to that of ' near.'"

4) Sobolewski, *De Praepositionum Usu Aristophaneo* (Moscow, 1890), p. 161: "Sed omnino genetivum multo usitatiorem dativo in quotidiano Atticorum sermone fuisse vel inde clarissime apparet, quod Aristoph. hoc usu ἐπί iungit dativo in senariis 11-ies, in alio genere versuum 13-ies (quo annumeravi etiam Vesp. 1293, ubi Aristoph. tragicos imitatur), genetivo autem in senariis 48-ies, in aliis numeris 14-ies." In a footnote he adds: "Errat igitur Rutherfordius, qui hunc dativi usum a comicis omnino abiudicat (Babrius, p. 7)." On the difference between gen. and dat., p. 160: "Quaerenti mihi, quid inter utramque constructionem interesset, sensus quidem discrimen esse nullum visum est," citing Eq. 783 by the side of 754, and Vesp. 1040 as compared with Lys. 575, 732, Eccl. 909.

5). Gildersleeve, *American Journal of Philology*, XI, p. 372, reviewing Sobolewski's book: "Under ἐπί c. gen. Sobolewski rejects Krüger's distinction between ἐπί c. gen. and ἐπί c. dat. in a local sense, a distinction which, it is true, might well be reversed theoretically as well as practically, for we should expect the natural position to be expressed by ἐπί c. gen., the unnatural by the dat. Fixity of position is in fact often denoted by ἐπί c. gen. (see my Justin Martyr, Apol. I 26, 15), and it is not impossible that there may be some such feeling as we have in regard to ὑπό c. gen. and ὑπό c. dat. In refutation of Krüger, Sobolewski points triumphantly to Eq. 783 compared with 754, but he might have claimed here, not mere indifference, but, if one must refine, reversal. It would be easy to make Demos wriggle in the one

---

[1] See, however, to take the word Mr. Rutherford himself has chosen, Lycurg. κατὰ Λεωκράτους §40 ὁρᾶν δ᾽ ἦν ἐπὶ μὲν τῶν θυρῶν γυναῖκας ἐλευθέρας περιφόβους κτλ.

passage and sit quiet in his 'fixed normal position' in the other. At any rate, the gen. is much more common in Attic daily speech than the dat., as Sobolewski shows, though, as he also notes, Rutherford is wrong in denying ἐπί c. dat. in this sense to Attic (Babrius, p. 7)."

6). Transferring the question to Homeric Greek (Monro, *Homeric Gram.*, §200) : "The gen. with ἐπί is used in nearly the same sense as the dat., but usually with less definitely local force; in particular—1) with words expressing the great divisions of space, espec. when a contrast is involved (land and sea, etc.); as ἐπὶ χέρσου, ἐπ' ἠπείρου, ἐπ' ἀγροῦ ; Od. 12, 27 ἢ ἁλὸς ἢ ἐπὶ γῆς ἀλγήσετε— 2) where the local relation is a familiar one ; as ἐπὶ νηός, ἐπ' ἀπήνης, ἐφ' ἵππων, ἐπὶ θρόνου, ἐπ' οὐδοῦ, ἐπὶ πύργου, ἐπ' ἀγκῶνος, ἐπὶ μελίης (ἐρεισθείς). Thus ἐπὶ νηυσί means *on* or *beside* ships, ἐπὶ νηῶν *on board* ships." (But for the Greeks before Troy was ἐπὶ νηῶν a more familiar location than ἐπὶ νηυσί?)

Further quotation is needless to prove variety of opinion.[1] Mr. Rutherford is perhaps alone in denying to Attic Greek prose the use of the dat. in the sense of superposition. This point is naturally the first to be taken up, and could perhaps be determined by an appeal simply to Att. Greek prose. But it will be better to present at the same time and in historic order the whole material of the question.

The following lists

1) include only concrete substantial things, admitting abstractions, metaphors or other unrealities only when they vividly suggest their originals, *e. g.* Soph. Ant. 189–90 (speaking of the πόλις) ταύτης ἔπι πλέοντες ; Ar. Av. 39–40 οἱ μὲν γὰρ οὖν τέττιγες . . . . ἐ. τῶν κραδῶν ᾄδουσ', 'Αθηναῖοι δ' ἀεὶ ἐ. τῶν δικῶν ᾄδουσι ; Xen. An. II 5, 23 of the wearing of the tiara ἐ. τῇ κεφαλῇ and also ἐ. τῇ καρδίᾳ.

2) exclude on the contrary concrete objects where evidently the meaning is not purely local, *e. g.* Z 423–24 πάντας γὰρ κατέπεφνε . . . . βουσὶ ἐπ' εἰλιπόδεσσι (cf. vv. 209, 221) ; Xen. Cyr. V

---

[1] I may, however, quote Kuemmell, *De Praepositionis ἐπι Usu Thucydideo* (1875), p. 30 : "Structuris Genetivi et Dativi collatis demonstrabo saepe fere nihil interesse Genetivus an Dativus sit usurpatus." He then compares I 13, 5 with I 56, 2, ἐ. τοῦ ἰσθμοῦ and ἐ. τῷ ἰσθμῷ ; II 93, 4 with VIII 106, 4 ἀκρωτηρίου and -ῳ ; IV 118, 4 with 105, 2 ἐ. τῆς αἰτῶν μένειν and ἐ. τοῖς ἑαυτοῦ . . . μένειν ; IV 100, 4 with VIII 69 1, ἐπ' αὐτοῦ (sc. τείχους) and ἐ. τείχει ; III 102, 4 (and IV 101, 3) with II 80, 2 (and IV 10, 3) νεῶν and ναυσί.

3, 34 *ἰ. τοῖς ὑποζυγίοις καὶ ὀχήμασι καταλιπεῖν τινα* ; Isoc. 17, 42 (ὁλκάδα) *ἐφ᾽ ᾗ πολλὰ χρήματ᾽ ἦν ἐγὼ δεδωκώς*, of a loan, not literally as Baiter translates it " navem onerariam, cui ego multas merces imposueram."[1] See p. 33

3) include, but keep separate, all instances where *ἐπί* with either case is equivalent to *at* or *near*.[2]

4) include those instances of *ἐπί* c. dat. after vv. of motion wherein a clear image is presented of superposition consequent upon the action of the verb.[3] Hence Π 579 *ἰ. νεκρῷ κάππεσεν* and the like are included, but not such instances as *ἐπ᾽ ἀλλήλοισιν ἰόντες* ' going at each other.' The verb of motion is always given in the lists (sometimes also other words which may aid the memory in recalling the passage).

5) exclude all temporal, causal, or other developed uses of *ἐπί* c. gen. and dat. The bearing, however, of such uses on the question will be shown later.

6) include reference to a few works undoubtedly of the post-classic age, *e. g.* the Batrachomyomachia, the spurious Platonic dialogues and others. There is still a remnant of respect for these works, though hardly justifiable.[4]

7) include, for convenience, under the department of History the dozen instances more or less to be found in Xenophon's philosophical works, since for him the department would hardly affect the style in this particular.

8) Instances of the case-form ·φι(ν), which is neither gen. nor dat., have been omitted altogether. They can offer little aid in establishing a difference of the cases, since it is only by that difference that their own usage is established.

9) Instances in the Att. Greek inscriptions down to 300 B. C. being few in number (12 of the dat. and 9 of the gen.) and not

---

[1] Attention will be occasionally drawn to the more striking or doubtful passages of this kind in the notes accompanying the lists, but a full account of the omissions is given in Appendix A.

[2] Yet it must be borne in mind that the Greeks said *upon* (*ἐπί*), and that this separation of the passages according to our translation or to our view of the facts of the case is only one of convenience in this special inquiry. The inquiry is, not the various meanings of *ἐπί* in English, but the translation of *upon* into Greek.

[3] See Kühner's Gram., §447, for this so-called *constructio praegnans.*

[4] See, for the probable date of the Batrach., Van Herwerden in *Mnemos.* New Series, X (1882), p. 171.

9

alw.iys of clear signification, are not included, but may be found in Append. B.

10) The lists are arranged according to the period and department of the authors, the words within the lists alphabetically. Substantives when given in the nominative do not stand in the passage cited, but some word of reference instead, which is always indicated. References in brackets, either by figures or abbreviations, indicate those other lists or authors in which the same word will be found but *in the other case*. For example, the bracket [3. 4. Hd. X.] after the word ὄρεσι in list 7 indicates that in lists 3, 4, and in Herodotus and Xenophon the word will be found *in the gen. case* c. ἐπί denoting superposition.

I.—EPIC.

a) *Iliad and Odyssey.*

ἐπί c. Dat. = *Superposition.*

αἴγειρος Δ 484 ἀκροτάτῃ.
αἵματι λ 82.
ἀκτῇ Β 395. ω 82. [Hm. 3. 6]
ἀπήνη ζ 75 κατέθηκεν. [Hm. Hs. 3]
ἀσπίς Λ 36 τῇ. [2. 3. Ar. Hd. X.]
βηλῷ Ψ 202 ἐπέστη.
βλεφάροισι Κ 26 ἐφίζανε. Ξ 165 χείη. α 364 βάλε. β 398 ἔπιπτεν. ε 271 ἔπιπτεν. μ 338 ἔχευαν. ν 79 ἔπιπτεν. π 451 βάλε. τ 590 χυθείη. 604 βάλε. υ 54 ἔχευεν. φ 358 βάλε. ψ 309 πῖπτεν. [3]
βωμός Θ 240 πᾶσι . . . μηρί' ἔκηα.
γ 273 βωμοῖς. [1. 2. 3. Ar. X. 6]
γαίῃ Γ 114 κατέθεντο. Λ 161. Ν 654 κεῖτο. Π 310 (*v. l.*) κάππεσε. 413 κάππεσε. Ρ 58 ἐξετάνυσσε. 85 κείμενον. Φ 118 κεῖτο. Ψ 876 πάγη (Nauck conj. ἐνί). κ 165 κατακλίνας. σ 92 τανύσσειεν. τ 200 ἵστασθαι (*v. l.* γαίης, which I prefer). Note that in all these passages γαίῃ stands at

end of verse, where corruption is easy. [1. 2. 3. 4. Th. X. 6. Pl.]
γούνασι Ζ 92 θεῖναι. 273 θές. 303 θῆκεν. Ι 488 γούνεσσι καθίσσας. Χ 500. τ 401 θῆκεν. φ 55 θεῖσα. [X. 6]
δίφρῳ Ζ 354 ἕζεο. τ 101 αὐτῷ κῶας ἔβαλλεν. [Hm. Hy. Hs. 4. X.]
δοῦρα *ship-timbers* μ 444 ἑζόμενος δ' ἐπὶ τοῖσι.
ἕλκεϊ Ο 393 ἔπασσε.
ἔστορι Ω 272 βάλλον.
εὐχάρη ζ 52 ἧστο. 305 ἧσται. η 153 κατ' ἄρ' ἕζετο. 160 ἧσθαι. ξ 420 ἕστησαν. υ 123. [X. 6]
θινί Δ 248. Ψ 59 κεῖτο. β 408. γ 5. η 290. ι 551. λ 75.
θρόνοισι π 408 καθίζον. [Hm. Hy. X.]
θρωσμῷ Κ 160 εἵαται. Λ 56. Υ 3.
ἱεροῖσι Λ 775 σπένδων. μ 362 λείψαι.

ἱπποῦν Ψ 362 μάστιγας ἄειραν. ο 182
μάστιν βάλεν. See notes at end
of this list.

ἱστός *mast* μ 422 αὐτῷ, βέβλητο.
[Hd.]

καρπῷ *wrist*(?) E 458. 883. Θ 328.
Ρ 601. Σ 594. Φ 489. Ω 671.
σ 258. χ 277. ω 398.

κλισμοῖσι Θ 436 καθῖζον = Λ 623 =
Ρ 90. [Hy.]

κόλπῳ Ζ 400.

κρατί Γ 336 ἔθηκεν. Ε 743 θέτο.
Κ 335 ἔσσατο. Λ 41 θέτο. Ο 480
ἔθηκεν. Π 137 ἔθηκεν. χ 123
ἔθηκεν.

κροταφοῖς σ 378 ἀραρυῖα = χ 102.
[4]

κώπῃ Α 219 σχέθε χεῖρα.

λίθοις Σ 504 εἵατο. γ 406 κατ᾽ ἄρ᾽
ἕζετο. 408 οἷς, ἵζεσκεν. θ 6
καθῖζον. [Ar. X.]

λιμέσι τε καὶ ἀκταῖς Μ 284 κέχυται.

λύγος ι 428 τῆς ἔπι Κύκλωψ εὗδε.

μαζῷ λ 448. τ 483. [Hd. μαστοῦ]

μελάθρῳ τ 544 κατ᾽ ἄρ᾽ ἕζετο.

μοχλός ι 382 ἄκρῳ.

μύλης η 104. [Hs.]

νεκρῷ Π 579 κάππεσεν. Ρ 300
πέσε.

νέκυς ψ 47 ἀλλήλοισι, κείατο.

νευρῇ Δ 118 κατεκόσμει ὀιστόν. Θ 324
θῆκε.

νηυσί Β 351 ἔβαινον. Ο 388. β 414
νηὶ κάθεσαν. ω 419 τιθέντες.
In Θ 222, Λ 5, 600, κ 408
whether superpos. or proximity is meant is uncertain.
[1. 2. 3. Ar. Hd. Th. X.]

ὄζῳ Β 312 ὄζῳ ἐπ᾽ ἀκροτάτῳ. [Eur.]

ὄιες Ε 141 ἀλλήλῃσι, κέχυνται.

ὄμμασι Κ 91 ἰζάνει. ε 492 χεῦε. [3]

ὄρεσσι Ε 523 ἔστησεν. See also
the list of proper names be-
low. [Soph. Ar. Hd. X.]

οὔδει Ε 734 κατέχευεν. Θ 385 κατέχευεν. Τ 92.

οὐδῷ (γήραος) Χ 60. Ω 487.
ο 348.

ὠσί μ 200 ἄλειψα.

ὀφρύσι Υ 151 καθῖζον (of a hill).
Of the face, ο 102. ψ 396.

ὄχθῃ Φ 17. [X.]

πέζῃ Ω 272 κατέθηκαν (ζυγόν).

πέτρῃ Π 407 καθήμενος. 429. [2.
Eur. Ar.]

πήχει (of a bow) φ 419.

προβώλῳ μ 251.

πύλῃσι Γ 149 εἵατο. Σ 275 σανίδες
ἐπὶ τῆς ἀραρυῖαι.

πύργῳ Γ 153 ἧντ᾽. 384. Ζ 431.
Χ 97 ἐρείσας. [Hm. Hs. Eur.]

ῥυμός Ε 729 ἄκρῳ δῆσε. Ω 271
ῥυμῷ, κατέθηκαν.

σάκος Η 246 αὐτῷ.

σκοπέλοισι μ 239 ἔπιπτεν.

στήθεσσι Δ 420. Ι 490. Μ 151.
Σ 317. Φ 254. Ψ 18 θέμενος.
727 κάππεσε.

σχίζῃς Λ 462. γ 459.

τάλαρος δ 134 αὐτῷ.

τείχεῖ Χ 463 ἔστη. [X. Cf. τειχίων
Eupolis]

τρόπις ἠδὲ καὶ ἱστός μ 425 ἱζόμενος
δ᾽ ἐπὶ τοῖς. [Hm. Eur.]

τύμβῳ Β 793 ἵζε. Λ 371. Ρ 434.
λ 77 πῆξαι.

φηγῷ Η 60 ἑζέσθην.

χειῇ *hole, den* Χ 93 (= *at*?).

χείλει (sc. τάφρου) Μ 51 ἐπ᾽ ἄκρῳ
χ. ἐφεστηότες. [Hd. Th.]

χερσί δ 213 χευάντων. ω 230.
[2. Hd.]

χθονί Α 88. Γ 89 ἀποθέσθαι. 195.
Δ 443. Ζ 213 κατέπηξεν (ἐνί
Bekker, Christ, Leaf, Faesi
and others). 473 κατέθηκεν.
Θ 73 ἐζέσθην. Μ 158 κατέχευεν.
Ρ 550. Σ 461. Υ 483 κεῖται.
Φ 426 κεῖτο. Ψ 731 κάππεσον.
α 196. ζ 153. η 67. 307.
θ 222. ι 89. λ 461. μ 191.
π 439. ω 535 πῖπτε. [1. 3]
χιτῶσι Φ 31.
χροΐ Ρ 210 ἥρμοσε.
ψαμάθοις Α 486 νῆα ἔρυσσαν. Ψ 853
ἔστησαν. γ 38 ἵδρυσεν. ν 119
ψαμάθῳ, ἔθεσαν. 284 ἐκείμην.
χ 387 κέχυνται.
ὤμοις ο 61 βάλετο. [Hm. 3. Hd.
6. Pl.]

*Proper Names and References
to Persons.*

Ἰφιδάμαντι Λ 261.
Καλλικολώνῃ Υ 53.
Ὄσσῃ λ 315 θέμεν.
Οὐλύμπῳ λ 315 θέμεν.
Πατρόκλῳ Ρ 706.
ἀλλήλοισι χ 389 μνηστῆρες ... κέχυντο. [Pl.]
αὐτῷ (of various persons) Ξ 419.
Π 661. Ω 666. Δ 470. Ρ 236,
where note contrast with ὑπό.
Ψ 381 (?). ω 525. Also in
the phrase ἀράβησε δὲ τεύχε'
ἐπ' αὐτῷ Δ 504. Ε (42). 58.
294. 540. Θ 260. Ν 187.
Ρ 50. 311. ω 525.
τῷ Ε 101 = 283 = 347. Ψ 188.
Ω 445 τοῖσι.

Despite varying opinion I have here and throughout put the words βωμός and ἐσχάρα under the head of superposition rather than of proximity. For whenever fire is mentioned, it is clearly a case of superpos., while elsewhere it must be borne in mind that the βωμός regularly presented a foundation *upon* which the sacrificers stood, and that the ἐσχάρα was in all likelihood surrounded with a paved space *upon* which, e. g. suppliants sat. Else why the mention of ashes in η 153 ὡς εἰπὼν κατ' ἄρ' ἕζετ' ἐπ' ἐσχάρῃ ἐν κονίῃσιν?

In ἱπποϊῖν of the above list Giseke in Ebeling's *Lex. Homer.* sees the genitive. And it is true that except once in Aesch. ἐπί always takes the genitive of this word. But βάλλω in ο 182 can hardly take the gen.,[1] nor would that construction be supported by the usage of ἐπιβάλλω (4 times in Hm.), for in the only passage where the gen. appears with it (z 68) the verb is in the middle voice.

In B 89 πέτονται ἐπ' ἄνθεσι, ἐπί is 'towards.' So too in Ψ 821 ἐπ' αὐχένι κῦρε. In η 120–21 ὄγχνη ἐπ' ὄγχνῃ γηράσκει, μῆλον δ' ἐπὶ μήλῳ, αὐτὰρ ἐπὶ σταφυλῇ σταφυλή, σῦκον δ' ἐπὶ σύκῳ, the image of superpos. is almost as strong (γηράσκει = πίπτει) as in the phrases μοῖραν (μόρον,

───────

[1] See *infra* p. 56

ἄλγεα, κῦδος, ὄνομα, κράτος) θεῖναι ἐπί τινι (Λ 509. E 384. Z 357. Ψ 400. 406. θ 554. λ 560. τ 592), or in ἐπὶ σώματι κύρσας (Γ 23). But in accordance with the classification they usually receive, I have omitted them from the above list. ἐπὶ προθύροισι (Σ 496. a 103) is also here and elsewhere regularly excised from the list of concretes, though I should prefer to follow Gerlach (*Philologus*, XXX, p. 503) in understanding by πρόθυρα a portico or covered space before the gates of the court. See, however, Buchholz, *Homerische Realien*, II 2, p. 96.

ἐπί c. Dat = Proximity.

ἐσχατιῇ β 391 στῆσε. ι 182. κ 96 (La Roche reads -ῆς, citing ι 280). [Hm. Pl.]

θύρῃσι B 788. σ 239 ἧσται. χ 250. ψ 49. [Hd. 6]

κάπῃσι Θ 434 κατέδησαν. δ 40 κατέδησαν.

κλησι[1] Π 170. β 419 καθῖζον = δ 579. θ 37 δησάμενοι. ι 103 καθῖζον = 179 = 471 = 563 = λ 638 = μ 146 = ο 221 = 549 = ν 76.

κρήνῃ ν 408. ο 442. [Hs.]

λίμνῃ Υ 390.

νηυσί A 559. B 4. Δ 513. E 791. Z 50. Θ 180 γένωμαι. 380. 531 ἐγείρομεν. I 425. K 306. 381. Λ 135. M 38. 90. 246. 403. N 107. 333 νέεσσι. 381. 762. 832. Ξ 51 νέεσσι. 57. 65. 367. O 44. 248. 459. 494. 722 νέεσσι. Π 18. 201. 547. Σ 7 κλονέονται. 259. 294. 304. T 71. 135 νέεσσι. 160. ΄ 236.

Φ 135. X 334. Ω 254. δ 248.[2] [Hm. 3. Ar. Hd. Th. X.]

ὁδῷ Z 15. M 168. Π 261.

πείρασι γαίης ι 284.

πηγῆs B 523. [Hm.]

ποταμῷ E 598. Θ 490 ἀγαγών. [X. 6]

προχοῇσι P 263.

πρυμνῇσι Θ 475. Ξ 32. Ο 385. Σ 76. 447. [Eur.]

ῥηγμῖνι A 437. Θ 501. δ 430. 575. ι 150. 169. 547. 559. κ 186. μ 6. ο 499.

ῥοῆς Π 719.

σταθμοῖσι ρ 20.

τάφρῳ Λ 48. 51. M 76. 85. Ξ 67 ῇ. [Hd.]

τεῖχος H 440 αὐτῷ. I 349 αὐτῷ. [X. Cf. τειχίων Eupolis]

φάτνῃ E 271. Z 506. K 568 κατέδησαν. O 263 (*Ety. Magn.* 51, 10 reads φάτνης). Ω 280. δ 535 = λ 411. Always at end of v. exc. in K 568. [4]

---

[1] κληῖδες = σκαλμοί, not ζυγά. So Doederlein, *Homerisches Glossarium*, §2115, followed by Eberhard in Ebeling's Lexicon, and by Buchholz, *Hom. Real.* II 1, p. 262.

[2] ἐπὶ νηυσί = *towards* after ἐλαύνειν (E 327. Λ 274. 400. O 259. Ω 392), φέρεσθαι (O 743), ἐγείρειν (O 603) and νίεσθαι (X 392).

Ἀλφειῷ Λ 712.
Ἀσωπῷ Κ 287.
Ἑλλησπόντῳ Η 86.   ω 82.
Κελάδοντι Η 133.
Ξάνθῳ Ε 479.

Σατνιόεντι Φ 87.
Σκαμάνδρῳ Ε 36 καθεῖσεν.
Ὕλλῳ Υ 392.
Ὠκεανῷ κ 511.   ψ 244.

The contents of this list should be noted, that its primitive concreteness may be compared with the wide development of the later period.   Nine words are the names of rivers, with which should be classed κρήνῃ, λίμνῃ, πηγῇς, ποταμῷ, προχοῇσι, ῥοῇς, τάφρῳ, as all denoting waters *upon whose margin* the subject stands. Now since the step from ἐπὶ χείλει τάφρου (a dat. of superpos.) to ἐπὶ τάφρῳ is an easy one, and since the image of superpos. remains as clear in the latter as in the former phrase, all the above words, as also ὁδῷ, could be entered without much forcing among the dats. of superpos., leaving the present list to consist of eleven words.   Of these eleven, ἐσχατιῇ and πείρασι (γαίης) might also readily join the other group, but that the superpos. of the one object upon the other, owing to the distance of the image called up, fades away and we descry only proximity.   Three others—κάπῃσι, φάτνῃ, κληῖσι—need historical interpretation.   As a consequence the list almost disappears, and ἐπί c. dat. in Homer when with concrete things is found to present almost invariably superposition.

To be excluded from both lists, because not purely local or not sufficiently concrete, are ἐπὶ βουσί Ζ 424. υ 209. 221. 363, κτεάτεσσι Ε 154. Ι 482. α 218. ο 89, ὄεσσι Ε 137. Ζ 25. Λ 106, σοῖσι β 369, φρεσί Α 55. Θ 218. ε 427. λ 146. ο 234. σ 158. φ 1, ἀνθρώποισι ν 60.

ἐπί c. Gen. = Superposition.

ἀγκῶνος Κ 80 ὀρθωθείς.   Π 702 βῆ (v. l. ὑπ').   ξ 494.
ἀγροῦ α 185 ἔστηκεν.   190.   π 330. 383.   χ 47.   ω 212. 308.
ἀκμῆς (ξυροῦ) Κ 173 ἵσταται.
ἄκρης θ 508 ἐρύσαντας.   [Th. X.]
ἀκτῆς Υ 50 -άων.   (Ψ 125 La Roche reads κὰδ δ' ἄρ' ἀκτῆς with six MSS.)   ε 82 καθήμενος.   151 καθήμενος.   κ 140 κατηγαγόμεσθα.   [I. 2. Eur.]

ἄμαξα Ω 190 αὐτῆς, δῆσαι.   267 αὐτῆς.   [Th.]
ἀπήνης Ω 275 νήεον . . . ἄποινα.   447.   ζ 252 τίθει.   [Hm.]
βωμῶν *bases* η 100 ἔστασαν.   [I. 2. 3. Ar. Hd. Th.]
γαίης Ν 565 (v. l. dat.).   μ 27 γῆς.   ξ 85 βῶσιν.   φ 41.   [I. 3. X. Pl.]
δίφρου Ω 578 κὰδ δ' . . . εἴσαν.   ρ 602 ἕζετ'.   τ 97 αὐτοῦ = φ 177 = 182.   ω 408 ἕζετ'.   [Hm.]

εἰνάων *mooring-stones* Ξ 77 ὁρμίσ-
σομεν.
ἠιόνος Ψ 61 κύματ' ... κλύζεσκον
(La Roche, *towards*).
ἡμιόνων *mule-car* Ω 702 κείμενον.
ἠπείροιο, -ου Α 485 ἔρυσσαν. α 162.
γ 90. ι 85 βῆμεν = κ 56. ξ 136.
π 325 ἔρυσσαν = 359. 367.
θρόναυ Α 536 καθέζετ'. Σ 389 καθεῖσεν. 422 ἷζε. Ω 522 κατ' ...
ἕζευ. ε 195 καθέζετ'. η 162 εἶσαν.
169 εἶσε. κ 314 εἶσε. 366 εἶσε.
σ 157 κατ' ... ἕζετ'. υ 96 κατέθηκεν. φ 139 κατ' ... ἕζετ' =
166 = ψ 164. [Hm.]
ἵππων *chariot* Ε 249. Μ 82. Σ 531
βάντες. Ω 356. (In Ρ 459 τοῖσι
is perhaps the Trojans.)
κορυφῆς Ν 12 ἧστο. Ξ 157 ἥμενον.
[2. Ar.]
λαμπτήρ τ 63 αὐτῶν, νήησαν.
μελίης Χ 225 ἐρεισθείς.
μηρός, -ίον Α 461 αὐτῶν δ' ὠμοθέτησαν
= Β 424 = γ 458 = μ 361.
νηῶν, -ός Ε 550 ἐπέσθην. [Θ 528
φορέουσι.] Ν 665 ἔβαινε. Π 223
θῆκ'. α 171 ἀφίκεο. 260 ᾤχετο.
β 322 ἰών. δ 489 ὤλετ'. 817
ἔβη. θ 500 βάντες. ι 535 ἔλθοι.
λ 115 νεῖαι. 508 ἤγαγον. 534
ἔβαινεν. μ 358. ν 216 οἴχωνται.
ξ 188 ἀφίκεο. 295 ἐέσσατο. 298
ἑπόμην. 357 ἔβαινον. ο 452
ἄγαιμ'. 547 ἔβη. ρ 160 ἥμενος.

249 ἄξω. τ 238 ἰόντι. 243 ἀπέ-
πεμπον. 259 ᾤχετ'. 339 ἰών.
φ 39 ἐρχύμενας. ψ 176 ἰών. ω 117
ἔπεσθαι. 301 εἰλήλυθας. [Hm.
3. 4. X. Pl.]
οὐδοῦ *threshold* α 104 στῆ. δ 718
ἷζε. κ 62 ἐζόμεθ'. ρ 339 ἷζε.
σ 33. χ 203 ἐφέστασαν.
ὀχέων Θ 455. [Hy. 3]
πήρης ρ 357 κατέθηκεν.
πύργων Θ 519 λέξασθαι. Ι 588 βαί-
νον. Μ 265. Π 700 πύργου ἔστη.
Φ 526 πύργου, ἑστήκει. All at
end of v. [Hm. 3. Hd. X.]
σανίδος φ 51 βῆ.
σαυρωτῆρος Κ 153.
σχεδίης ε 33. 163 αὐτῆς, πῆξαι.
338 ἷζε. η 264. 274. [X.]
τελαμών Λ 38 αὐτοῦ (*v. l.* αὐτῷ),
ἑλέλικτο δράκων.
τράπεζα Λ 629 αὐτῆς (*v. l.* -τῇ).
[4. Cf. 6. Pl.]
τράπιος τ 278. [Hm.]
χέρσου Ξ 284 βήτην. κ 459 = λ 401
= 408 = ω 111. τ 278 ἔκβαλε.
ω 291. All at end of v.
χθονός Γ 293 κατέθηκεν. Υ 345
κεῖται (Barocc. χθανί). τ 470
ἐξέχυθ'. [1. 2. 3]
ὤμων Α 46. κ 170 ὤμου. [Hm. 3]

Βουπρασίου Λ 756 βήσαμεν (La
Roche, *towards*).

ἐπὶ νηῶν in Ε 700 (προτρέποντο μελαινάων ἐπὶ νηῶν) means 'toward
the ships.'

ἐπί *c. Gen = Proximity.*

ἐσχατιῆς ε 489 (*v. l.* dat.). σ 358.
[Hm. Hs. 2. 6]
κρατός (λιμένος) ι 140. ν 102. 346.
ὄγμου Σ 557 ἑστήκει.

πηγαί Χ 153 αὐτάων, πλυνοί ... ἐγγὺς
ἔασι. [Hm. X. Pl.]
χέρσου η 278 βιήσατο κῦμα. ο 495
λύον ἱστία.

ἐπ' ἐσχατιῆς ι 280 (ἔσχες .... νῆα) is perhaps best taken with La Roche as 'toward.' So περάαν (περνὰς) νήσων ἔπι Φ 454, X 45, though Giseke in Ebeling's Lexicon has them = *supra, in*. Too problematic to be included is α 278 = β 197 ἕεδνα) ὅσσα ἔοικε φίλης ἐπὶ παιδὸς ἕπεσθαι. For the forms in -φιν, see p. 8.

It will be observed that in this last list, as with the datives of prox., the image of superpos. is still clear, *on* answering almost as well as *at* even in English.

b) ˙ Hesiod and the Homeric Hymns.

ἐπί c. Dat. = Superposition.

ἀκταῖς Sc. 213 ἧστο. Hy. 7, 3 ἀκτῇ. [Hm. 3. 6]

αὐχένι 5, 217 κεῖται. [3]

βλεφάροις Hs. Frg. 5, 4 πῖπτεν. [Eur.]

βουσί Op. 434 ἄροτρον . . . βάλοιο.

βωμοῖς Op. 136 ἔρδειν. [1. 2. 3. Ar. X. 6]

γαίῃ 3, 339. [Hm. 2. 3. 4. Th. X. 6. Pl.]

γλώσσῃ Theog. 83 χείουσιν. [2]

γούνασι Epigr. 4. Batr. 3 θῆκα. [X. 6]

ἔργοις *fields* Op. 549 ἀήρ . . τέταται.

ζώνῃσι Sc. 233 ἀπηωρεῦντ'.

ἠλέκτρῳ Epigr. 15, 10.

θειμέλια 2, 117 αὐτοῖς, ἔθηκε.

θεμέθλοις [Theog. 816].

καρήνοις Sc. 236 ἐδονεῖτο . . . φόβος.

καρπῷ *wrist* 2, 18.

κολωνῷ 5, 272, 298. [Hd.]

κρατί Sc. 136 κυνέην ἔθηκε. 6, 7 ἔθηκαν.

κροτάφοις Sc. 137 ἀραρυῖαν. Batr. 131. [4]

μέλεσσι Theog. 152 = 673 ἐπέφυκον = Sc. 76 = Op. 149.

μῦς Batr. 91 αὐτῷ.

νώτῳ Op. 544 ἀμφιβάλῃ. [Hd. Th.]

οὔδει 3, 149, 284 καθίσσαι.

οὐδῷ (γήραος) Op. 331.

ὄχθῃς, -ῃσι, -αις Batr. 166 ἔστησαν. 223. 247. [X.]

[ὄχοισι 5, 19 at end of v. "Iam Vossius, postea Grashof, ὀχεσφιν pro ὄχοισιν scribendum esse iure censuerunt." Ebeling's Lex., s. v. ὄχος (2).] [Hm.]

πεδίῳ 2, 42 στῆς.

πέτρῃ Sc. 406. 375 ἀλλήλῃς. Hy. 3, 124, 404. [2. 3. Ar.]

πλαταμῶνι 3, 128 εἰρύσατο.

πόντῳ 2, 216.

προσώπῳ 10, 2. [Hs. 4. 6]

σήματι Epigr. 3. [Hd.]

τύμβῳ Epigr. 3.

ὕδατι Batr. 74. 99. (In v. 61 ἐν should be read with 3 MSS, Matthiae, and Franke. In v. 89 ὑφ', Bothe's correction, is necessary to the sense). [Hd.]

χθονί Theog. 556. 564. Sc. 162. 462 κάββαλε. Op. 90. 157. 252. Frg. 14, 4. [1. 2. 3]

ψαμάθοις 2, 329 ἐρύσαντο.   3, 79   ἀλλήλοις Sc. [379] πέσον, sc. ἄνδρες.
ἔρριψεν.   [7]
ὠλένῃ 3, 388.   αὐτῷ Batr. 205 ἀρόβησε δὲ τεύχε'
                                                       ἐπ' αὐτῷ.
Ἀγχίσῃ 4, 170 ὕπνον ἔχευε.

ἐπί c. Dat. = Proximity.

ἐσχατιῇ Theog. 622 εἶατ'. Frg.   ῥεέθροις 1, 18.
   156, 5. [Hm. Pl.]   ῥηγμῖνι 2, 312, 327, 330.
θύρῃσι 3, 26. Epigr. 11. [Hd. 6]
κρήνῃ 19, 20. [Hs.]   Ἀλφειῷ 34, 3.
πείρασι 4, 227.

Excluded from both lists are βουσί Theog. 290. Hy. 3, 200, 316,
556. προβάτοισι 3, 571. φρεσί 2, 197, 356. 4, 15 because either not
purely local or not concrete. Op. 750 μηδ' ἐπ' ἀκινήτοισι καθιζέμεν
is of problematic meaning, while in Op. 162 Rzach reads ὑφ'
instead of ἐφ'.

ἐπί c. Gen. = Superposition.

ἀδάμαντος Sc. 231.   νηός Theog. 998 ἄγων. Op. 236
ἀπήνης Sc. 273. [Hm.]   νηῶν, νίσσονται. Hy. 2, 316
βωμῶν Theog. [557]. [1. 2. 3.   ὄρουσα. 7, 10 εἶσαν. 45. [Hm.
   Ar. Hd. Th.]   3. 4. X. Pl.]
δίφρων Sc. 306 βεβαῶτες.   321   προσώπου Sc. 147. [Hy. 2. 4. Pl.]
   δίφρου, θόρε. Hy. 5, 198 δίφρου, πύργων Sc. 242. [Hm. 3. Hd. X.]
   ἧστ'. [Hm.]   σέλματος 7, 47. [3]
ἠπείρου Op. 624 ἐρύσαι. Hy. 2, 310   χθονός 1, 133. 20, 3. [1. 3]
   ἐρύσασθε. 7, 22 ἀφῶμεν.   χώρης 3, 123 κεῖτ'.
θρόνου 4, 165 κατέθηκε. [Hm.]
κλισμοῖο 5, 193 ἐδριάασθαι. [Hm.]   Δήλου 1, 49 ἐβήσατο.   115 ἔβαινε.
κρηνάων Op. 758 οὐρεῖν. [Hm. 2.   Κύνθου 1, 141 ἐβήσαο.
   Hd. X.]   Τελφούσης 2, 62 βῆς (sc. γῆς ? Cf.
μύλης Frg. 228 ἀλετρεύουσι. [Hm.   Δήλου, Βουπρασίου Λ 756).
   2]

There seem to be no cases where ἐπί c. gen. denotes proximity.

2.—LYRIC.

ἐπί c. Dat. = Superposition.

αἰετός Pind. P. 1, 7 Fοι, ὕπνον κατέχευας.
ἀκταῖσι Pind. P. 4, 36 θορών. [Hm. 3. 6]
ἄνθεσι Solon 25.
αὐχένι Theogn. 1357 ζυγόν . . . κεῖται. [3]
βλεφάροισι Phocyl. (? See Bergk, II, p. 72) κάθηται. Theogn. 208 ἕζετο. Pind. Py. 9, 24 γλεφάροις. [3]
βωμῷ Pind. O. 6, 70. (The MSS show no iota. Boeckh, however, says that Pind. did not use the gen. in ω.) Pind. Frg. 129 -οῖς. [1. 2. 3. Ar. X. 6]
γαστρί Archil. 72 προσβαλεῖν.
γλώσσῃ Theogn. 85 ἐ. γλ. τε καὶ ὀφθαλμοῖσιν ἔπεστιν | αἰδώς. Pind. O. 6, 82 δόξαν ἔχω τιν' ἐ. γλ. ἀκόνας λιγυρᾶς. [2]
δενδρέῳ Pind. Frg. 230 βαίνειν. [Hd.]
εὐναῖς Pind. P. 9, 12 βάλεν. [X.]
κορυφαῖς Critias 7, 9 καθίζῃ. ⌊Hm. X.]
κρημνοῖς Pind. O. 3, 22 'Αλφεοῦ. [Hd.]
λεχέεσσι Pseud.- Phocyl. 189. [Eur.]
ὁδῷ Pind. O. 10, 30.

ὕσδῳ Sappho 93. [Eur.]
ὅσσοις Sappho 29 ἀμπέτασον.
ὀφθαλμοῖσι Theogn. 85. See γλώσσῃ supra.
ὀφρύσι Anacr. 54 θέμενοι.
ὄχθαις Pind. P. 12, 2. N. 9, 22. [X.]
παρῇσι Phrynicus 2.
πετάλοισι Ibycus 8.
πέτραις Simonid. 58, 2 ναίειν. [2. 3. Ar.]
προσώπῳ Sappho 100 κέχυται. [Hs. 4. 6]
στήλῃ Pseud.-Simonid. 183, 4.
σφυρῷ Pind. Is. 7 (6), 13 ἕστασας. [2]
χείλεσι Plato 1, 1. 32, 7 βαῖνον. [Cf. Hd. Th. χείλεος τάφρου]
χθονί Theogn. 799. Archil. 56, 2. [Aristot.] 5, 12. [1. 3]

Ἴδᾳ Pind. N. 10, 71 πλάξε κεραυνόν.
ἀλόχῳ Pseud.-Phocyl. 186 χεῖρα βάληαι.
ἀνέρι Cleobulina 1 κολλήσαντα.
παιδί Pseud.-Phocyl. 210 τρέφειν χαίτην. Ion 1, 7 ἄλλῳ, πέσῃ.
τοῖσδεσι (sc. πράγμασι) Critias 4, 3 σφραγὶς δ' ἡμετέρης γλώσσης ἐπὶ τοῖσδεσι κεῖται.

ἐπί c. Dat. = Proximity.

δίνῃσι Anacr. 1 Ληθαίου.
ἐσχάρῃ Semonid. Amorg. 7, 47 ἐσθίει. [X. 6]
ἐσχατίαισι Alcaeus 69. [Hm.]

θύραις Pind. N. 1, 19 ἕσταν. [Hd. 6]
κράνᾳ Pind. P. 4, 294. [Hs.]
λίμνῃ Theogn. 7. [Hd.]
μύλᾳ Alcman 70. [Hs.]

πόλεσι Carm. Popul. 44. [3]
προχοῇσι Solon 28. Aristot. 53
ἔθεσαν. Simonid. 120.
ῥεέθροις Pind. O. 13, 35. N. 9, 9.
Is. 5 (4), 33.
ῥηγμῖνι Pind. N. 5, 13.
τύμβῳ Theogn. 1203 οἰμωχθείς.

ὕδατι Pind. N. 3, 4. [Hd.]

Ἀλφεῷ Pind. O. 8, 9.
Εὐρίπῳ Pind. P. 11, 22.
Εὐρώτᾳ Theogn. 1088 ποταμῷ.
Κασταλίᾳ Pind. P. 4, 163.
Κηφισσῷ Aristot. 21 ποταμῷ θέσαν.

Archil. 131 χολὴν γὰρ οὐκ ἔχεις ἐφ' ἥπατι gives no longer a concrete image, hence is excluded.

ἐπί c. Gen. = Superposition.

ἀγροῦ Bacchyl. 49, 1.
ἀκμῆς (ξυροῦ) Theogn. 557. Simonid. 97, 1.
ἁρμάτων Hippon. 42, 1 ἐφ' ἁρ. τε καὶ Θρηΐκίων πώλων | λευκῶν ἰών. Pind. O. 1, 77. [3]
ἀσπίδος Tyrtae. 11, 31 ἐρείσας. Pind. P. 8, 46. [Hm. 3]
ἀτράκτω Adesp. 52 (MS -τῳ).
βαθμῖδος Pind. N. 5, 1 ἑσταότ'.
βωμῶν Bacchyl. 13, 3. [1. 2. 3. Ar. Hd. Th.]
γῆς Tyrtae. 10, 31 στηριχθείς = 11, 22. [1. 3. X. Pl.]
γλώσσης Theogn. 815 βοῦς . . . ἐπιβαίνων. Adesp. 87 -ας. [Hs. 2. 3]
ἀϊόνων Sappho 30.
θάκω Alcman 87 ἧστ'. So Bergk. [3]
ἵππου Corinna 14, 1. [3]

λευκίππων (sc. ἁρμάτων) Anacr. 12 B.
νηῶν Simonid. 105, 3. [Hm. 3. 4. X. Pl.]
ξύλου Carm.Popul. 34, 3 καθημένην.
ὁλκάδος Pind. N. 5, 2.
πέτρας Carm. Popul. 46, 25 καθήμενος ("circa Ol. 122, 3," Bergk). [1. 2. 3. Ar.]
πώλων Hippon. 42, 1. See ἁρμάτων supra.
ῥινός Herodas 4 μή . . . τὴν χολήν . . . ἔχ'. MSS ῥῖνας.
ῥυτίδων Plato 30, 2 ἔπεστιν ἔρως.
σφύρων Sappho 70 τὰ βράκε' ἕλκην. [2]
τραχήλου Adesp. 22 βαῖνε.
χειρός Theogn. 490 (doubtful). [Hm.]
χώρας Pind. P. 4, 273. [Hd.]

There seems to be but one passage in which proximity might be denoted, though here, too, superposition is better, viz. πόντου ἐπ' Εὐξείνου Simonid. (? See Bergk, III, p. 516.)

3.—TRAGEDY.

ἐπί c. Dat. = Superposition.

ἀγκύλαις Iph. A. 615 δέξασθε.
Iph. T. *1250*.[1] Ion 761 λαβεῖν.
ἀκταῖς Pers. *963* ("fortas. ἀγαῖς,"
Wecklein). Hec. 28. 36.
698. Hipp. 1179 (Kirchh.
and Wilam.-Mollend. ἀκτάς).
Andr. *1018* -αῖσι. Hel. 609
-αῖσι. 739. Iph. A. 807. Iph.
T. 272. 932. Eur. Frg. 636,
2. [Hm. 3. 6]
ἄντυγι Rhes. *236* βαίη (ἄντυγα?).
ἄξυσι Phoen. 1194 ἐπήδων ἄξονες.
ἅρματι Phoen. 1110 σφάγι' ἔχων.
[2. 3. Ar. Hd. X. Pl.]
ἀσπίδι Phoen. [1120]. 1124 ἐπί-
σημα. [2. 3. Ar. Hd. X.]
βοστρύχοις Bacch. 757 πῦρ ἔφερον.
βωμοῖς Aesch. Suppl. *694* θείατ'.
Alces. **133**. [1. 2. 3. Ar. X. 6]
γᾷ Ant. *134* πέσε. [Hm. 2. 3. 4.
Th. X. 6. Pl.]
γλώσσῃ Ag. 36 βοῦς. Aesch. Frg.
316 κλῄς. O. C. *1052* κλῄς ...
βέβακε. [2]
δέλτῳ Iph. A. **155**.
δεμνίοισι Cycl. *499*.
δέρῃ Orest. 1653.
δύμοις Med. *1270* πίτνοντ' ... ἄχη.
[3]
ἕρκει *bezel of ring* Trach. 615
ὄμμα θήσεται.
ἐσχάρᾳ Eum. 108. [X. 6]
ζυγῷ *bench* Ag. 1618. Phoen.
74 καθέζετ'. *yoke* Heracl. 854
σταθέντ'. Rhes. 766.
θάκοις Iph. A. *195*. [2]

ἵπποις Aesch. Frg. 38 ἐμπεφυρμένοι. [2. 3. Ar. Hd. X. 6. Pl.]
κάρᾳ Bacch. 833. Troad. 937.
καρπῷ *wrist* Ion 1009.
κοντῷ Alces. *254* ἔχων χέρ' ...
Χάρων.
κράνει Eur. Elec. *470*. [Cf. κρανίου 4]
κρατί Ant. *1345* εἰσήλατο. Med.
1065. Bacch. 831. Hel. *372*
χέρας ἔθηκεν. Herc. Fur. *640*
κεῖται. [Hm.]
νηΐ Phil. 891 οὑπὶ νηΐ ... πόνος.
Hel. *1135* ναυσί, νεφέλαν (*i. e.*
Helen) ἄγων. Iph. T. *1109*
(MSS ἐν). [1. 2. 3. Ar. Hd.
Th. X.]
νώτῳ Aesch. Suppl. *90* πίπτει.
Hel. 774 πόντου. 842 τύμβου.
984 τύμβου. [Hd. Th.]
ὄμμασι Aj. 51 βαλοῦσα. O. C. *1685*
βέβακε. Phoen. 950 βαλών.
[3]
ὀμφαλῷ Eum. 40. [Pl.]
ὅσσοις Hec. *915*. Alces. 269
ἐφέρπει.
ὀφθαλμοῖς Sept. 403 πέσοι. Iph.
A. 5.
ὄχθῳ Heracl. *781*. (For Choeph.
4 see *infra*.) [Cf. ὄχθαι X.]
ὄχοις Prom. 710 ναίουσι. Troad.
569. [Hm.]
παρῇσι Phrynicus 13.
πασσάλῳ Hec. *920*. [Ar.]
πέδῳ Heracl. 75 χύμενον.
πέτραις Bacch. 306. [2. 3. Ar.]

---

[1] Italic figures denote lyric, black figures anapaestic passages.

πυρί Ion 707.
πύργοις Ag. 357 ἔβαλες. [1. 3]
ῥοθίῳ Iph. T. 425 δραμόντες.
σέλμασι Sept. 32 στάθητε. [Hy.]
σκήπτροις Ag. 75. Orest. 1058.
  [Ar.]
σκοπέλοισι Ion 871. 1479.
σμικροῖς O. C. 148 ἐ. σμ. μέγας
  ὥρμουν.
σποδᾷ Ant. 1007 ἐτήκετο.
στέρνοις Ion 995.
σώματι Cho. 723. [3]
τάφῳ Orest. 471 χοὰς χεόμενος.
  Hel. 986 κεισύμεσθα. [Hd. 6]
τοίχοισι Ion 1158.
τρίποδι Orest. 164.
χθονί Trach. 811. Hec. 486.

Med. 434 ξένᾳ ναίεις χθ. Herc.
Fur. 849. Iph. A. 1587. [1. 3]
χρωτί Ant. 246 παλύνας.
ψαμάθοις Hipp. 235.
ὤμοις Trach. 564 φέρων. Phoen.
  1131 φέρων. Bacch. 755 ἔθεσαν.
  Eur. Frg. 863 φέρων. [Hm.
  3. Hd. 6. Pl.]
ἀλλήλοισι Pers. 506 πῖπτον. O. C.
  1620 ἀμφικείμενοι. [Pl.]
γυνή Aj. 1295 ἐφ' ᾗ λαβών ... ἄνδρα.
'Ιλιάσι Androm. 301 ζυγὸν ἦλυθε.
μοί Trach. 981 βάρος.
παρθένοι O. C. 1611 αὐταῖς, πτύξας
  ... χεῖρας.
σοί Eur. Elec. 1344 ἴχνος βάλλουσι.

ἐπί c. Dat. = Proximity.

δρόσοις Iph. A. 182 κρηναίαισι.
δώμασι Orest. 1255. Phoen. 1533.
ἐσχάραις Alces. 119. [X.]
ἱστοῖς loom Bacch. 514.
κώπῃ Alces. 361. 439 -ᾳ.
λαίφεσι Troad. 690.
μελάθροις Herc. Fur. 691.
νεκρῷ Aj. 1319.
ὅπλοις Eur. Suppl. 674.
παγαῖς Eur. Frg. 773, 33.
πόλει Trach. 246 βεβώς (local
  signif. is sufficient). [3]
πύλαις Prom. 729. Sept. 631.
  Ant. 141. Aj. 49. Alces. 100.
πυρᾷ Troad. 483. [3]

ῥηγμῖσι Iph. T. 253.
ῥοαῖς Phoen. 574. Hel. 52. 124.
  Eur. Elec. 1273. Eur. Frg. 14.
σκηναῖς Aj. 3. Hec. 733.
σποδῷ O. T. 21.
στεφάνοισι Phoen. 786.
σφαγῇ Hel. 1582 ταυρείῳ, σταθείς.
τεράμνοις Hipp. 536.
τύμβῳ Eur. Elec. 1326.
χεύμασι Phoen. 793.

Κυκλωπείοισι Herc. Fur. 998.
Σιμόεντι Troad. 810.
Τροίᾳ Phil. 353. 611.

It is not certain whether superpos. or proxim. should be understood in Choeph. 4 τύμβον δ' ἐπ' ὄχθῳ τῷδε κηρίσσω πατρί, and in
Soph. Frg. 342 μέδεις εὐανέμου λίμνας ἐφ' ὑψηλαῖς σπιλάδεσσι (of Posei-
don). The readings are corrupt in Herc. Fur. 1003 ἐ. λόφῳ κέαρ,
Hipp. 1195 ἐφ' ἅρματι, while in Eur. Frg. 628 ἐπ' ἐσχάραις Ammo-
nius' citation has ἐσχάρας. To the words regularly excluded, as

21

ἐξόδοις, προθύροις, τέρμασι, τόποις—for which see Append. A, 5—must be added Λυδοῖς Trach. 356, λουτροῖσι Soph. Elec. 445, ψυχῇ Ant. 317, ῥιπῖσι Soph. Frg. 511, στεφάνοισι Phoen. 831, κερκίσι Ion 506, in which there is either lack of concreteness, doubt in interpretation, or remoteness of metaphor. In Aesch. finally must be noted ἐπί in the sense of *towards* or *for* in Sept. 423, 714, 1059, Suppl. 1003, Frg. 69.

ἐπί c. Gen. = *Superposition.*

ἀγκύρας Hel. 1071. [Cf. σμικροῖς O. C. 148]

ἀγρῶν O. T. 1049. Eur. Elec. 623.

ἀκμῆς Hel. 897.

ἄκρων (sc. δακτύλων) Aj. 1230. [Cf. X.]

ἀκτῆς, -ᾶς Pers. 449. 965 θείνοντας. Phil. 272. Hec. 778 (ἀκταῖς of the same fact in v. 698). Iph. T. 1170. [1. 2. 3]

ἀπήνης O. T. 802 ἐμβεβώς [Hm.]

ἅρματος Aesch. Frg. 38. [3] See *infra.*

ἀσπίδος Sept. 387. 400. 478. 510. 512. 520. 559. 661. [Hm. 3]

ἀστράβης Adesp. 210.

αὐχένων Pers. 191 τίθησι. (Orest. 51 ἐπ' αὐχένος βαλεῖν is spurious. See p. 57.) [Hy. 2. Hd. Pl.]

βαλβίδων Ant. *132.*

βλεφάρων Eur. Suppl. *284.* [1. 2]

βωμοῦ Androm. 1123 ἔστη. Note Heracl. 238 Ζεύς) ἐφ' οὗ σὺ βώμιος θακεῖς. [1. 2. 3. Ar. Th.]

γῆς Soph. Elec. 1136. Aj. **235** γαίας. O. T. 113. 416. O. C. *1705* γᾶς. *1712.* Orest. 233 γαίας, ἁρμόσαι πόδας. Hipp. *763* ἔβασαν. Alces. **869** πόδα πεζεύων. Hel. *525* πόδα χριμπτόμενος. Troad. 884. [1. 3. X. Pl.]

γραμμή Eur. Frg. 382, 9 ἐπ' αὐτῆς τρεῖς κατεστηριγμέναι (i. e. 'E').

δόμων Orest. 1574 ἄκρων. [3]

δορός *ship* Androm. *793.*

ἕδρας O. C. 85.

ἑστίας Ag. 1435. [6]

ἵππων Pers. **18.** Eur. Frg. 675. [Aesch.]

κανόνος Agathon Frg. 4 ἐφ' ἑνός.

κλίμακος Iph. T. 1382 θορών (Wecklein reads accus.). [X.]

κρηπίδων Herc. Fur. 1008 ἔκειτο. Ion 38 τίθημι. [X.]

λᾶος O. C. *195.*

λέχους Orest. 313 μένε. [2]

ναῶν *temples* Eur. Elec. 6 τέθεικε.

νεώς Pers. **18** ναῶν. Phil. *516.* 648. Iph. T. 102. 1000. Rhes. 72 θρώσκων. 97 νεῶν. [Hm. 3. 4. X. Pl.]

νήσου Phil. 613 ἧς ναίει.

ξένης O. C. *184.* 563. Androm. *136.*

ξυροῦ Aesch. Frg. 99, 22 ἔβην (so Wil.-Mollen.). Ant. 996. Herc. Fur. 630 ἔβητ'.

ὄζων Bacch. 1070 ἱδρύσας. [Hm. 2]

ὀμμάτων Ag. *1428.* Eur. Suppl. 286 βαλοῦσα. Phoen. 1452 τίθησι. [Hm. 3]

ὀρόφων Aesch. Suppl. *651.*

ὄρεων O.T. *1105*. [Hm). Hd.X.Pl.]　　ῥώμης Orest. 68 ὀχούμεθα.
περγάμων Iph. A. *762* στάσονται.　　σκαλμῶν Iph. T. 1347.
πέτρας Eur. Suppl. 1045. [1. 2.　　σώματος Ag. *1472*. [3. 7]
　　3. Ar.]　　τρόπις Hel. 412 ἐφ' ἧς ἐσώθην.
πέτρου O. C. 19.　　　　[Hm.]
πύλεος = γῆς Androm. *137*.　　χέρσου Aesch. Suppl. 178.
πρύμνης Iph. T. 1377 σταθέντες.　　χθονός O. C. 1256. Med. 781.
　　[Hm.]　　　　Cycl. 543 θείς. [1. 2. 3]
πυρᾶς Eur. Elec. 513. Ion 1258　　χώματος Hec. 524 ἄκρον, ἔστησ'.
　　(troch. tetram.) ἵζε. [3. 6. Pl.]　　　Orest. 116 στάς. [X.]
πύργων Phoen. 1091 ἄκρων. [Hm.　　χώρας Trach. 300. [Hd.]
　　3. Hd. X.]　　ὤμων Soph. Frg. 344. Orest.
πώλου O. C. 312 βεβῶσαν.　　　　1532 (troch. tetram.). Eur.
ῥιπός Eur. Frg. 397 πλέοις.　　　　Elec. 813 ἦραν. Rhes. 305.
ῥοπῆς Hipp. 1163. [Cf. Th. and　　　[Hm. 3]
　　Pl., also gen.]

In Aesch. Frg. 38 cited above *s. v.* ἅρματος corruption seems almost a certainty. See Blaydes on Aristoph. Ran. 1403. Ant. 1141 ἔχεται πάνδαμος πόλις ἐπὶ νόσου, even with the aid of Hdt. 6, 11 ἐπὶ ξυροῦ γὰρ ἀκμῆς ἔχεται ἡμῖν τὰ πρήγματα, does not convey to all scholars the image of superpos., Jebb preferring to compare ἐπ' εἰρήνης. In Med. 135 ἐπ' ἀμφιπύλου γὰρ ἔσω μελάθρου γόον ἔκλυον Weil drops ἐπί, by which " on rétablit à la fois le sens et le mètre," and Verrall asks why ἐπί may not mean 'in the direction of,' 'toward.' For Cycl. 384 κορμοὺς πλατείας ἐσχάρας βαλὼν ἔπι see p. 56 . In Eur. Suppl. 272 γουνάτων goes of course with ἀντίασον, and in Trach. 1275 the reading is uncertain. This is the sum of the exclusions. For ἐπί c. gen. denoting proximity there are no examples.

4.—COMEDY.

a) *Aristophanes.*

ἐπί c. Dat. = *Superposition.*

ἄνθεσι Eq. *403*.¹　　　　κύτος θώρακος Pax 1235 δεκάμνῳ.
γόνασι Thesm. 1182. [X. 6]　　λυχνείῳ Frg. *561*.
κλάδεσι Av. *238*.　　　　μήλοις *i. e. breasts* Eccl. *903*.
κοίταις Vesp. **1040**.　　ὀφθαλμῷ Lys. *1026*. Ran. 1247
κορυφαῖς Nub. **270**. [Hm.]　　　-οῖς.
κροκωτῷ Ran. 46.　　　　πέτραις Eq. **783**. [2. 3. Ar.]

¹ Italic figures denote lyric, black figures anapaestic passages.

πλευραῖς Vesp. 1293. [Pl.]
προλόγοισι Ran. 1246.
σῆμα Thesm. 886 ἐφ' ᾧ. [Hd.]
τραπέζῃ Ach. *1158*. [4. Hd.]
ὑγρᾷ Vesp. **678**.
χείλεσι Ran. *679*. [Cf. Hd. and
   Th. χείλεος τάφρου]

χειρί Frg. 387, 10. [2. Hd.]
Ταινάρῳ Ach. 510.
ἀλλήλοισι Pax 901. [Pl.]
ἐμαυτῷ Ran. 9 ἄχθος . . . φέρων.
οἷς Plut. 185 ἐπικαθέζηται.
σοί Ran. **1046** 'πεκάθητο.

ἐπί c. Dat. = Proximity.

ἀναπαύλαις Ran. 195.
βωμοῖς Lys. 1140 ἱκέτης καθέζετο.
   [1. 2. 3. X. 6]
δημοσίοισι Eccl. **627**.
δρυφάκτοις Vesp. **552**.
θύραις Eccl. 865. 997. 1114.
   Ran. 163. Nub. *469*. Vesp.
   362. **1482** θάσσει. [Hd. 6]
κημοῖς Vesp. **754**.
κιγκλίδι Vesp. 124.
κουρείοισι Plut. 338.

οἰκίαισι Vesp. 801.
πύλαις Eq. 1246. 1247. 1398.
ῥοαῖσι Thesm. 864.
στόματι Eccl. 1107 τῆς ἐσβολῆς.
τραπέζῃ Pax **770**. [Hm. 4. Hd.]
τύμβῳ Ran. 1139.

'Αρταμιτίῳ Lys. *1251*.
Ληναίῳ Ach. 504 (Sobolewski,
   on).
Παλλαδίῳ Frg. 585.

Sobolewski is sure that ἐπ' ἐσχάραις Av. 1232 means *at*, not *on*.
I prefer to class it here, as doubtful; also ἐ. κώπαις Eq. 546, as
lacking satisfactory analogies. ἐπ' ὄχθῳ Ran. 1172 belongs to
Aesch., see tragedy *supra*. Examples such as Pax 123 κολλύραν
μεγάλην καὶ κόνδυλον ὄψον ἐπ' αὐτῇ are not usually reckoned as purely
local. See Append. A, 1.

ἐπί c. Gen. = Superposition.

ἀκμῆς Plut. 256 (iamb. tetram.).
ἁμάξης Plut. 1014 ὀχουμένην. [Th.]
ἀνθράκων Frg. 68. 135.
ἅρματος Eq. 968. Ran. 1403
   (from Aesch.).
ἁρμαμαξῶν Ach. 70.
ἀσπίδων Ran. 928 ἐπόντας (iamb.
   tetram.). [1. 3]
βήματος Plut. 382.
βωμός Pax 938 ἐφ' ὅτου. Cf. Eq.
   1312 'πὶ τῶν σεμνῶν θεῶν (troch.
   tetram.). [1. 2. 3. Th.]

γῆς Pax 896. \ [1. 3. X. Pl.]
δικῶν (as κραδῶν) Av. 41.
ἐλπίς (as a ship) Eq. 1244 ἐφ' ἧς
   ὀχούμεθα. Frg. 150, 11 ἐ. λεπτῶν
   ἐλ. ὠχεῖσθ'.
ἵππων Lys. *679*. [Aesch.]
κανθάρου Pax 81.
κελήτων Lys. 60.
κεφαλῆς Eccl. 222. Av. **487**.
   515. Plut. 1198. [Hd. X. Pl.]
κλίνης Lys. **575**. 732. Eccl. *909*.
   [Pl.]

24

κορήματος Frg. 474.
κραδῶν Av. 40.
κρεμάθρας Nub. 218.
λίθος Vesp. 332 ἐφ' οὗ. [Hm.]
λόφων Av. 293 (troch. tetram.).
[X.]
λυχνιδίου Frg. 281.
μελίας Av. 742.
μηρίων (as βωμῶν) Thesm. 693.
νεώς Ran. 52. [Hm. 3. 4. X. Pl.]
ξύλου Nub. 1431 (iamb. tetram.).
Vesp. 90.
ὀλίγου Lys. 31 εἴχετο. Cf. ἀγκύρας.
ὁρῶν Ach. 82. [Hm. Hd. X. Pl.]
παττάλου Vesp. 808. [3]
περιδρόμου balcony Frg. 133.
πέτρας Eq. 754. 956. Av. 836
-ῶν. [1. 2. 3. Ar.]

πίνακος Plut. 996 ἐπόντα. [Cf.
πινακίσκοις 4] .
προσώπου Nub. 1176. [1. 2. 4. Pl.]
πυγιδίων Ach. 638 ἄκρων.
ῥιπός Pax 699 πλέοι.
σκήπτρων Av. 510. [3. Hd.]
στρούθου Lys. 723.
τέγους Vesp. 68. Nub. 1502.
Frg. 11. Lys. 389 τεγῶν. 395.
τόνου Lys. 923.
τραπέζης Eq. 771. [4. Cf. 6 and
Pl. = bank]
τροχοῦ Lys. 846. Pax 452. Plut.
875.
τυροκνήστιδος Lys. 231.

Θράκης Lys. 103. Av. 1369. Pax
283. Ach. 602. Vesp. 288.

Eq. 1312 καθῆσθαι . . . . ἐ. τῶν σεμνῶν θεῶν has been admitted in
the above list, s. v. βωμός; see also Th. I 126, 11 and Eur. Heracl.
238.[1] Eccl. 496 ἐ. σκιᾶς ἐλθοῦσα, besides lacking concreteness, is
doubtful in reading, Von Velsen preferring ὑπὸ σκιάς and Sobolewski following him.
Genitives of proximity seem entirely wanting.

b) *Comic Fragments.*

ἐπί c. Dat. = *Superposition.*

ἄμβωσι Ephip. 5, 16 (Kock's
Com. Frgs. II).
ὀμύλοις Pherecr. 108, 17 (I). Pollux reading -ων. Telecleid.
32 (I) -φ.

ἑκατόμβαι Antiph. 164 (II) τούτοις
(sc. βουσί) ἐπετέθη.
ναυσί Hermipp. 63, 11 (I) hexam.
[1. 2. 3. Ar. Hd. Th. X.]
ὀδῷ (γήρως) Menand. 671 (III).

[1] In such phrases as εἰς (ἐκ, ἐν) διδασκάλου, Πυθίου, γείτονος, the explanation
by ellipse seems now to be losing favor. Vogrinz, for instance, Hm. Gram.,
p. 314, takes εἰς (ἐς) directly with 'Αίδαο, 'Αθηναίης, γαλόων, etc., where the
gen he says expresses "etwas der Person Zugehöriges, ihr Anhaftendes."
See, too, Schmalz, Lat. Gram., §113, Richard Meister, Die griechischen
Dialekte II, p. 297 ff. In the present case therefore (ἐ. θεῶν the prep.
according to this theory goes immediately with the gen. Rather than that,

πινακίσκοις Pherecr. 108. 14 (I).
Pollux reading -ων. [Cf. πίνακος Ar.]

προσώπῳ Eubul. 98, 7 (II). [Hs.
4. 6]

σανδάλια Cephisod. 4 (I) ἐφ' οἷς
. . . ἔπεστιν.

τραπέζῃ Philem. 17 (II) κείμενον.
Telecleid. I, 7 (I) -αις. [Hm.
4. Hd.]

χείλεσι Eupol. 94, 5 (I) ἐπεκάθιζεν.

τῷδε (sc. ᾠῷ?) Cratin. 108 (I)
ἐπώζουσ'.

ἐπί c. Dat. = Proximity.

θύραις Eubul. 53 (II). [Hd. 6]
λαχάνοις vegetable-market Cratin.
49 (I).
πορνείοισι Xenarch. 4, 4 (II).

τηγάνοις Pherecr. 127 (I).

Σάγρᾳ Alexis 305 (II).

Proximity is perhaps also in Hermipp. 53 (I) ὥρα μάττειν ἐ. τοῖς
ἱεροῖς. Menand. 1091 (III) seems corrupt. With Theopomp. 64
(I) κατακείμενοι μαλακώτατ' ἐ. τρικλινίῳ may be compared Eur. Phoen.
1533 ἐ. δώμασι.

ἐπί c. Gen. = Superposition.

ἁμαξῶν Menand. 396 (III).
Adesp. 497 -ης. [Th.]
ἀνθρακιᾶς Cratin. 143 (I) hexam.
(Porson's emend.).
ἀνθράκων Ophel. 1 (I).
βήματος Menand. 1121 (III).
γῆς Adesp. 352. [1. 3. X. Pl.]
δίφρου Menand. 877 (III). [Hm.]
ἑστίας Adesp. 463. [6]
κιόνων Crates 15 (I).
κόπρου Menand. 544, 5 (III).
κοχωνῶν Crat. 27 (I) τὰς τρίχας
καθειμέναι.
κρανίου Cratin. 71 (I). [Cf. κράνει 3]
κροτάφων Plat. 84 (I) ἄκρων. [Hm.
Hs. Batr.]

μαθήματος Amphis. 3 (II) ἑστηκώς,
as on a ship.
ξύλου Alex. 222, 10 (II). Hermipp. 9 (I) οὑπὶ τῶν ξύλων (prob.
not here official. See Append.
A, 2).
προσώπου Anaxandr. 58 (II). [2.
4. Pl.]
τειχίων Eupol. 207 (I). [τείχει 1.
Th. X. 6]
τηγάνου Eubul. 76 (II). [4]
τράπεζα Alex. 261, 3 (II) ἐφ' ἧς
ἐπέκειτ'. [4. (6. Pl.)]
τροχοῦ Theophil. 7 (II).

Θρᾴκης Adesp. 1219.

I should prefer the elliptic theory, or better yet, say that θεῶν, διδασκάλου,
etc., were *new indeclinable* substantives (in the gen. with ἐκ, dat. with ἐν,
acc. with εἰς), the neuter subst. διδασκάλου, etc., presenting a notion as distinct from that called up by διδάσκαλος as e. g. cashmere the stuff is distinct
from Cashmere.

ἐπί c. Gen. = Proximity.

φάτνης Adesp. 719, from Photius. [Hm. X.]

Menand. 202 (III) *ἐ. τοῦ σανιδίου* is problematic, Epinic. 1, 1
(III) is corrupt, but has been emended by Cobet, *Mnemos.* IV
322, who reads *ἐπαλφιτοῦτα* for *ἐπ' ἀλφίτου πίνοντα.*

5.—HISTORY.

a) *Herodotus.*

ἐπί c. Dat. = Superposition.

ἄκρῳ 4, 195. 7, 85. [X.]
ἀκρωτηρίῳ (τοῦ ὄρεος) 7, 217 ἐγένοντο.
    [Th.]
αὐχένι (τοῦ Βοσπόρου) 4, 118. [Cf. 3]
βάθρῳ 2, 176. [Hd. 6. Pl.]
βωμῷ 4, 35. [1. 2. Hd. X. 6]
δόρασι 7, 41.
ἡμιπλινθίον 1. 50 *ἐ. τούτοισι . . .*
    ἵδρυτο.
κανέῳ 1, 119.
κεφαλῇ 5, 12 (cf. gen. in same
    cap.).   Plur. in 5, 49. 7, 70,
    72, 74, 75, 76, 79, 84. [4. Hd.
    X. Pl.]
μετώπῳ 3, 28.

οἰκήματα 2, 148 ἐκείνοισι. [X. 6]
οἰκοδομήματι 2, 121 *a.*
ὄρεσι 2, 12. [3. 4. Hd. X.]
οὐδῷ (γήραος) 3, 14.
πυρί 9, 120.
πυραμίδες 2, 149 ἀμφοτέρῃσι. [X.]
πύργῳ 1, 181 (2) ἐπιβέβηκε. [1. 3]
ῥίῳ 4, 85.
σκήπτρῳ 1, 195 ἔπεστι. [Ar.]
τρίποσι 5, 59.
χώρῃ 5, 77. [2. 3]

Γεραιστῷ 9, 105.
Ταινάρῳ 1, 24.

ἐπί c. Dat. = Proximity.

διασφάγι 3, 117 πύλας . . . ἔστησε.
θαλάσσῃ 2, 159 (2). 3, 17. 4, 13,
    172. 6, 20, 118. 7, 89. [Hd.
    Pl.]
θύρῃσι 3, 16. [Hd. 6]
κρήνῃ 9, 51 *ἐπ' ᾗ.* [Hs.]
λουτρά 7, 176 αὐτοῖσι.
πόλι 6, 7 νῆσος . . . κειμένη. [3]
ποταμῷ 1, 189. 2, 103, 108. 4, 18,
    86, 124. 5, 13, 52 (3 ᾧ ἔπεισι,
    αὐτῷ, ᾧ), 119. 7, 124, 154. 9,
    16. See also list of proper
    names. [X. 6]

πρόπυλα 2, 91 αὐτοῖσι.
πύλῃσι 1, 89.
στόματι 2, 154. 4, 51, 53, 81, 87.
Ἀρτεμισίῳ 7, 183. 8, 21 (2), 42
    (2), 43, 45, 46 (2), 66, 76. 9,
    98.
Ἀσωπῷ 9, 19, 30, 38, 43.
Θερμώδοντι 4, 110. 9, 43.
Ἴστρῳ 4, 80.
Λάκαινα χώρη 7, 235 ἐπ' αὐτῇ νῆσος
    ἐπικειμένη.
Λήμνῳ 7, 6 νῆσοι ἐπικείμεναι.

Λιβύη 4, 153 νῆσος, 156, 195.   Σουνίῳ 6, 87.
Πελοποννήσῳ 3, 59 νῆσον.   Τριοπίῳ 7, 153 νήσου.
Σκαμάνδρῳ 5, 65.   Ὑπάνι 4, 53.
Σκιάθῳ 8, 92.   Ὠκεανῷ 4, 8.
Στρυμόνι 7, 25, 75. 8, 118.

In 8, 110 ἐ. τῷ πλοίῳ and 123 ἐ. τῷ βωμῷ it is doubtful whether ἐπί
means *on* or *at*; in 5, 121 τὴν ἐ. Μυλάσοισι ὁδόν it means *to*.

ἐπί c. Gen. = Superposition.

ἀγκυρέων 6, 12 ἔχεσκε. 7, 188 ὥρμεον.
ἀγορῆς 5, 89.
ἀγρῶν 1, 17, 120 -οῦ. 6, 23.
ἀκμῆς (ξυροῦ) 6, 11.
ἁμάξης 1, 31. 9, 80 -έων.   [Th.]
ἅρματος 7, 40, 100.   [3]
ἀσπίδος 9, 74.   [Hm. 3]
βάθρων 7, 23.   [Hd.]
βωμοῦ 1, 183 (2, θύειν and καταγί-
   ζουσι). 2, 39 ἐπ᾽ αὐτοῦ σφάζουσι.
   6, 81 θύειν, 97 ἐθυμίησε.   [Hd.
   Th.]
γεφυρέων 7, 54.
δακτύλων 6, 63.
δελφῖνος 1, 23, 24 ἐπέων.
δενδρέων 2, 32 ἐπεύντος.   [2]
ζευγέων 1, 199. 4, 46.
ἠιόνος 2, 113. 7, 44.
ἰκρίων 5, 16.
ἵππου 2, 162. 3, 86 -ων. 4, 64 -ων,
   110 τούτων, 116 -ων. 5, 112.
   9, 44.   [Aeschl.]
ἱστοῦ *mast* 8, 122.   [1]
καταστρώματος 8, 118 ἐπεόντων, 119.
κεφαλῆς 2, 35 -έων. 5, 12 (dat. in
   same cap.).   [Hd. X. Pl.]
κλίνης 1, 182.   [Pl.]
κνάφου 1, 92.
κολωνοῦ 7, 44.   [Hs.]
κρημνοῦ 4, 103.   [2. Th.]
κρυστάλλου 4, 28.

κυματωγῆς 9, 100.
λόφου 2, 124 (2), 127.   [X.]
μηχανῆς 2, 125.
μαστοῦ 3, 133.   [Hm.]
νεός, -ῶν 5, 33 (2), 36 ἐπιπλέοντας.
   6, 15 ἐπιβατεύοντας, 43 ἐπιβάς.
   In 7, 96, 181, 184 ἐπεβάτενον.
   8, 92 ἐπ᾽ ῆς, 118 ἐπιβάς.   [1. 3.
   4. X. Pl.]
νώτου 2, 68. 3, 28.   [3. Hs. Pl.]
ξύλα 1, 186 ἐπ᾽ ὦν. 4, 64 -ων, 103
   -ου.
ὄνων 2, 121γ ἐπιθεῖναι.
ὄφιος 9, 81 ἐπεστεώς.
ὀρέων 7, 111.   [Hm. Hd. X. Pl.]
ποίη 1, 132 ταύτης ἔθηκε.
πλοίων 1, 205.
πρώρης 7, 180.
πυρῆς 1, 86. 7, 167.   [6. Pl.]
ῥάχιος (τοῦ ὄρεος) 3, 54 ἐπεόντα.
σηκοῦ 4, 62.
σήματος 1, 93 ἄνω.   [Hm. & Ep. 4]
σταυρῶν 5, 16.
στιβάδος 4, 71.
στοίχου 2, 125.
συμβολῆς (of ζωστήρ) 4, 10 ἄκρης.
τάφου 5, 47 ἱδρυσάμενοι.   [3. 6]
τάφρου 4, 201.   [Hm. Th. X.]
τράπεζα 6, 129 αὐτῆς ὠρχήσατο.   [4.
   Cf. 6. 7]
ὕδωρ 3, 23 αὐτοῦ ἐπιπλέειν.   [Batr. 2]

ὑπωρέης 9, 19.   Θρήκης 6, 33.
χείλεος (ποταμοῦ) 2, 70. 4, 141.   Χερσονήσου 6, 39.
   [Hm. Cf. 2. 4]   παῖδες 2, 107 ἐκείνων ἐπιβαίνοντας.
χειρός 2, 141. [Hm. 4]
ὤμων 1, 209 (2). 2, 35. [Hm. 3]

ἐπί c. Gen. = Proximity.

γωνίης 1, 51. 8, 122.   Βόσπορος 4, 87 αὐτοῦ.
θαλάσσης 3, 5. [Hd. Th. X. 6.
   Pl.]
θυρέων 3, 120. 5, 92 γ. [1. 2. 4.
Hd. X. 6. Pl.]

ἐπ᾽ οἰκήματος 2, 121 ε, 126 would seem to belong here, yet historical knowledge on the matter might give the phrase, at least for some early period, its literal meaning. See Append. A, 6. In κύλπον τὸν ἐ. Ποσιδηίου 7, 115 the prep. is *toward*. For the official gen. τοὺς ἐ. τούτων ἐπεστεῶτας 4, 84 see Append. A, 2.

b)   *Thucydides.*

ἐπί c. Dat. = Superposition.

αἰγιαλοῖς I 7, 1. [X.]   τείχει VIII 69, 1. [Th. X. Cf.
ἄκραις VII 34, 2. VIII 106, 4 -ᾳ.   τειχίων 4]
   [Hm.]
ἀμάξῃ IV 67, 3. [1. 4. Hd. X.]   Αἴτνῃ III 116, 1.
βωμός VI 3, 1 ἐφ᾽ ᾧ θύουσι. [1.   'Επιπολαῖς VI 97, 4. 102, 1.
   2. 3. 4. Hd. X. 6. Cf. τῶν θεῶν   Λευκίμμῃ I 30, 1. 47, 2.
   I 126, 11]   'Ρίῳ II 84, 4. V 52, 2.
ἰσθμῷ I 56, 2. [Th.]   ἀλλήλοισι II 52, 2. VII 85, 1.
κρημνοῖς VI 97, 5 ἄκροις. [Hd.]   87, 2. [Pl.]
ναυσί IV 10, 4. [1. 2. 3. Ar. Hd.
   Th. X. 6]

ἐπί c. Dat. = Proximity.

θαλάσσῃ I 58, 2. II 9, 4. IV 26,   1. 78, 3, 5. 102, 1. VI 65, 1.
   2. 54, 1. 57, 1. VI 2, 6. VII   VII 35, 1, 2. 78, 3 αὐτῷ. 80,
   4, 2. [Hd. Pl.]   5, 6. 84, 2 αὐτῷ. [X. 6]
λιμέσι III 6, 2. IV 54, 4 λιμένι.   στόματι I 29, 3. 55, 1. IV 49.
πολίχνῃ VII 4, 6.   75, 2. 102, 4. VIII 90, 4.
ποταμῷ I 100, 1. III 99. IV 50,   τάφρῳ III 24, 2. [Hd.]

χωρίον VII 34, 2 ἐφ' ᾧ ὥρμουν.   Λαβδάλῳ VI 97, 5.
[Th.]   Λακωνικῇ IV 54, 4 νήσου ἐπικειμένης.

Λᾷ VIII 91, 2.
Αἰγίνῃ I 105, 2.   Λέσβῳ III 16, 1.
'Αρτεμισίῳ III 54, 4.   Λευκίμμῃ I 51, 4.
Δάσκωνι VI 66, 2.   Λοκροῖς II 32 νῆσος. III 89, 3.
Δηλίῳ IV 101, 5. V 14, 1. 15, 2.   Μιλήτῳ VIII 26, 2.
'Ερετρίᾳ VIII 60, 1.   Πύλῳ IV 14, 5. 28, 3.
Κεκρυφαλείᾳ I 105, 1.   Σκιώνῃ IV 131, 3. 133, 4 αὐτῇ.
Κερδυλίῳ V 6, 3, 5.   Στρυμόνι I 98, 1.
Κρήναις III 106, 3.   Τροπίῳ VIII 35, 3.

In four passages it may be doubted whether superpos. or proxim. be meant, viz. 'Ακτίῳ I 30, 3. Λευκίμμῃ I 30, 4. νήσῳ IV 55, 1. 'Επιπολαῖς VII 45, 1. Two instances are excluded because lacking concreteness, viz. IV 105, 2 ἐ. τοῖς ἑαυτοῦ μένειν. VIII 86, 3 ἐ. τοῖς σφετέροις αὐτῶν μένειν. For the official ἐ. ναυσίν of II 80, 2 see Append. A, 2.

ἐπί c. Gen. = Superposition.

ἀγκυρῶν VII 59, 2.   ξύλα VI 101, 3 αὐτῶν.
ἀκρωτήριον II 93, 4 αὐτοῦ. [Hd.]   πλοίου VI 61, 7. 88, 9.
γῆ (vel χώρα) IV 118, 4 ἐ. τῆς αὐτῶν   ῥοπῆς V 103. 2.
   μένειν. [1. 3. X. Pl.]   σχεδιῶν VI 2, 4. [X.]
ἰσθμοῦ I 13, 5. [Th. X.]   τείχους IV 32, 2. 100, 4 αὐτοῦ.
καταστρωμάτων I 49, 1, 3 -ος. VII   V 7, 5. VII 28, 2. [Th. 6]
   62, 1. 67, 2.   χείλους (τῆς τάφρου) III 23. 2, 4.
λόφων III 97, 2. 105, 1 -ου. IV   χωρίων III 97, 2. IV 102, 2 ἐφ'
   42, 2 αὐτοῦ. 128, 2. 129, 4 -ου.   οὗ. [Th.]
   131, 1 -ου. V 7, 4 -ου. [X.]
μετεώρου IV 36, 2. V 6, 3.   'Επιπολῶν VII 43, 4.
ναῦς II 23, 2 αὐτῶν. 56, 2 -ῶι. 57,   Θράκης I 56, 2. 57, 5. 59, 1. 60,
   1, -ῶν. 92, 3 -ός. III 8, 1 -ός.   3. 68, 4. II 9, 4. 29, 4, 5.
   102, 4 -ῶν. 115, 5 -ῶν. IV   58, 1. 67, 4. 79, 1. 95, 1, 2.
   101, 3 -ῶν. VI 37, 1 -ῶν. 91,   IV 7, 3. 78, 1. 79, 2. 82. 102,
   4 -ῶν. VII 25, 1 αὐτῶν. 71, 5   1. 104, 4. 122, 2. V 2, 1. 12,
   -ῶν. VIII 74, 1 αὐτῆς. [1. 3.   1. 21, 1. 26, 2. 30, 2. 31, 6.
   4. Th. X. Pl.]   35, 3, 5. 67, 1. 80, 2. 83, 4.
νώτου IV 4, 2. [Hs. 3. Pl]   VI 7, 3. 10, 4. VIII 64, 2.
ξηροῦ I 109, 4.

For I 126, 11 καθεζομένους .... ἐ. τῶν σεμνῶν θεῶν see *supra* p. 24.

ἐπί c. Gen. = Proximity.

φυλακτηρίου IV 110, 2.　　　　Λακωνικῆς V 34, 2 κείμενον.

c) Xenophon.

ἐπί c. Dat. = Superposition.

αἰγιαλῷ Hell. II 4, 8 κατέστησαν.
[X.]
ἄκρᾳ Hell. I 6, 26 Μαλέᾳ. De
Venat. 4, 8 -αις τρίχας ὀρθὰς (sc.
κύνες ἔχουσι). [1]
ἄκρῳ An. III 4, 49. IV 5, 1 ἐφ'
ᾧ. V 2, 16 -οις. VII 3, 44 -οις.
Hell. V 4, 14. De Venat. 10,
2 -οις (sc. ἀκρολινίοις). [3]
ἀκρωμίᾳ De Re Eq. 6, 7 κατατιθέτω.
γῇ De Venat. 12, 6. [1. 2. 3. 4.
Th. X. 6. Pl.]
γόνασι Cyr. VII 3, 5. [X. 6]
ἰσθμῷ Hell. V 2, 15. [Th.]
καρδίᾳ An. II 5, 23.
κεφαλῇ An. II 5, 23. V 4, 13. VII
4, 4 -αῖς. [4. Hd. X. Pl.]
κλίμαξι Hell. VII 2, 8. [3. X.]
κρηπίς An. III 4, 10 ταύτῃ, ἐπῳκο-
δόμητο. [3. Pl.]
λόφῳ An. VI 3, 22. Hell. VI 2,
7. 4, 4. VII 4, 26. [4. Hd.
Th. X.]
νάπει An. VI 5, 22 γέφυρα ἦν.

νευραῖς An. V 2, 12 ἐπιβεβλῆσθαι.
νηΐ Hell. IV 3. 12. [1. 2. 3. 4.
Hd. Th. X. 6]
ὁδῷ An. IV 1, 20. 2, 6 ἐφ' ᾗ, 7.
6, 26. Cyr. V 3, 52.
οἰκίαις An. IV 4, 2 ἐπῆσαν.
ὄρεσι Hell. VI 5, 18 συλλεγομένους.
Ages. 2, 4 -ει. [3. 4. Hd. X.]
ὀφρύσι καὶ ταῖς οὐραῖς De Venat. 4, 8
ὄχθαις An. IV 3, 3. [X.]
πύργος Cyr. VI 1, 54 αὐτῷ. [1. 3]
στήλῃ Cyr. VII 3, 16 ἐπιγεγράφθαι.
σχεδίαις An. II 4, 28. [Hm. Th.
Pl.]
τείχεσι An. I 4, 4 ἐφεστήκεσαν.
[τειχίων 4]
φρεατίᾳ Hell. III 1, 7 ἐπέστησεν.
χώματι Hell. II 3, 46. [3]
ὑψηλοτάτῳ (τῷ) De Vect. 4, 44.
[X.]

'Ονείῳ Hell. VI 5, 51.
Γραὸς στήθει Hell. V 4, 50.
αὐτῷ An. I 8, 27 ἔκειντο.

ἐπί c. Dat. = Proximity.

ἀνδρῶνι Conv. 1, 13 στάς.
ἄρκυσι Cyr. II 4, 25.
ἀρχείοις Cyr. VII 7, 85.
βασιλείοις Cyr. VII 5, 26.
δρυφάκτοις Hell. II 3, 50 ἐπιστῆναι.
3, 55.

θαλάττῃ An. I 4, 1, 6. V 3, 2.
5, 2. VI 4, 4 (2). VII 1, 28.
2, 36, 38. 3, 16. 6, 43. Cyr.
VII 4, 9. Hell. I 4, 3. IV 8,
26. [Hd. Pl.]

31

θύραις An. I 9, 3. II 4, 4. 5, 31
(2). III 1, 2. VI 5, 23. VII
3, 16. Cyr. I 3. 2. VI 1, 1.
VIII 1, 33, 34. 6, 10. 8, 13.
Hell. III 1, 28. [Hd. 6]
κρήνη An. I 2, 13 ἐφ᾽ ᾗ. [Hs.]
λιμένι Hell. II 1, 23. VI 2, 7
ἐφώρμει.
νάπῃ Hell. V 4, 44 ἐγίγνοντο.
νάπει An. VI 5, 12 ἐγένοντο.
πηγαῖς An. I 2, 8. [Hm.]
ποταμῷ An. I 3, 20. Cyr. VII 5,
11. [X. 6]
πύλαις An. I 4, 5. VII 1, 17.

σκηναῖς Cyr. IV 2, 32. VII 5, 6
ἐγένοντο.
στόματι An. III 4, 43 τοῦ πλαισίου.
Cyr. II 4, 25 -σι τῶν πόρων.
Hell. III 1, 23 στρατεύματος.
τάφρῳ An. I 7, 19. [Hd.]
φάτνῃ Cyr. III 3, 27 -αις. De
Re Eq. 5, 1. [4]
χαράδρᾳ An. III 4, 1 ἐφ᾽ ᾗ. IV 2, 3.

Δηλίῳ Mem. III 5, 4.
Καδμείᾳ Hell. VI 5, 46.
Λεύκτρῳ Hell. VI 5, 24.
αὐτοῖς Hell. V 4, 59.

ἐπί c. Gen. = Superposition.

ἀγροῦ Hell. II 4, 27. VI 2, 6 -ῶν.
αἰγιαλοῦ An. VI 4, 1. [Th. X.]
ἄκρων An. I 2, 21. IV 6, 18. V
2, 1. 4, 26 -ου. Cyr. III 2, 4
-ου. VIII 7, 3. Hell. IV 6, 11
ἀκροτάτου. VII 2, 11 -ου. [Hd.
X.]
ἁμαξῶν An. I 7, 20. II 2, 14 -ης.
Cyr. VII 3, 1. [Th.]
ἀναβολῆς An. V 2, 5.
ἀνώγεων An. V 4, 29.
ἅρματος An. I 2, 16. 7, 20. Cyr.
III 3, 43. VI 1, 50. VIII 3,
13. [3]
ἁρμαμάξης An. I 2, 16. 2, 18.
Hell. III 1, 13.
ἀσπίδων Hell. IV 4, 10. [Hm. 3]
βωμῶν Mem. I 1, 2. Apol. 11.
[1. 2. 3. 4. Hd. Th.]
γῆς An. III 2, 19. Cyr. IV 5, 54
καταπίπτοντες. V 2, 15. VII 5,
12. De Venat. 5, 8 ἑαυτῆς. 5,
13. 6, 25 ἑαυτῆς. [1. 3. X. Pl.]
γήλοφος An. I 10, 12 ἐφ᾽ οὗ. III

4, 28 -ου, 44 -ου. Hell. VII 5,
24 -ων, κατέστησεν.
γονάτων Conv. 9, 4 ἐκαθέζετο. [1. 4.
X. 6]
διφθέρα An. I 5, 10 τούτων.
δίφρου De Re Eq. 7, 5. [1]
δόρατος Cyr. VII 1, 4.
ἐσχάρας Cyr. VIII 3, 12. [1. 2. 3]
εὐνῶν Cyr. VIII 8, 19. [2]
ἐφιππίου De Re Eq. 7, 5.
θρόνου Cyr. VI 1, 6 ἐκαθέζετο.
Hell. I 5, 3 ἐφ᾽ οὗ. Conv. 9, 3
ἐκαθέζετο. [1]
ἱππαρίων Cyr. I 4, 19.
ἵππου, -ων An. III 2, 19. 4, 47,
49. VII 3, 26 οὗ. 4, 4. Cyr.
I 3, 3. 4, 7, 25. III 3, 27. IV
1, 11. 3, 14, 20. 5, 49, 54, 58.
6, 1 (2). V 2, 1, 17. VIII 3,
15. 8, 19. Hell. V 2, 29. VI
4, 11. Ages. 2, 25. De Re
Eq. 7, 5. 8, 10. 9, 9. 11, 8.
12, 1. Mag. Eq. 6, 5. 8, 13.
[Aesch.]

κώμηλοι Cyr. VI 2, 18 ὧν. VII, 1
48 αὐτῶν.
κανώθρου Ages. 8, 7.
καταστρώματος Hell. I 4, 18.
κεφαλῆς An. IV 3, 6. Cyr. III
3, 66 τῆς τάφρου. Cf. χείλεος
τάφρου. [Hd. X. Pl.]
κλίμακος An. IV 5, 25. [X.]
κορυφῆς An. IV 2, 20 ἐγένοντο. [2]
λίθος De Re Eq. 4, 4 τούτων. [1]
λόφου An. IV 2, 13. VI 3, 11, 12.
5, 28. Cyr. VII 3, 5. [X.]
μνημάτων Hell. III 2, 14. [6. Pl.]
ναῶν Hell. VII 4, 32.
νεῶν An. I 4, 3. Hell. I 6, 35
αὐτῶν. 7, 32 -ώς. IV 8, 21.
[1. 3. 4. Th. X. Pl.]
νήσων Hell. V 1, 2 ποὶ ἀφιγμένος.
ξένης De Rep. Lac. 14, 4.
οἰκήματος Cyr. VI 1, 53 -ων. Hell.
IV 5, 6. [Hd.]
ὀρέων An. IV 1, 11. 3, 7 -εος. 7,
21 -εος, ἐγένοντο. 8, 9 -εος. VII
4, 11 -εος. [1. Hd. X. Pl.]
ὀχήματος An. III 2, 19. Hell. III
4, 19 -ων. Ages. 1, 28 -ων.
ὄχθαι An. IV 3, 5 ὧν. [1. 2. X.
Cf. ὄχθος 3]

πέλτης An. I 10, 12.
πηλοῦ Oec. 19, 14 ἄνω καταθείης.
πυραμίς An. III 4, 9 ταύτης. [Hd.]
πύργων Cyr. VII 1, 39 ἀναβῆναι.
[X.]
ῥαπτά Hell. IV 1, 30 ὧν.
στιβάδος Cyr. V 2, 15.
ταπίδων Cyr. VIII 8, 16 τιθέασιν.
τειχῶν An. VI 2, 8. Cyr. V 2, 2.
Hell. IV 4, 12. VII 2, 8. [1.
Th. 6]
τεύχους Hell. I 7, 11.
τριήρων An. VI 2, 14. Hell. V
4, 56 -οιν. VI 4, 18 ὧν.
τροχός Conv. 7, 2 οὖ. 7, 3 -οῦ.
ὑψηλοῦ Hell. IV 5, 4. De Re
Eq. 12, 11. [X.]
χιόνος An. IV 5, 19.
ὠμοπλάται De Venat. 5, 30 αὐτῶν.

Θράκης An. VII 6, 25. Hell. I 3,
17. II 2, 5. V 2, 12, 24.
Νοτίου Hell. I 5, 14 τρόπαιον στῆσας.
αὐτῶν (sc. ἃ ἡ γῆ φύει) De Venat.
5, 8 κατακλίνονται.
ἑτέρου (sc. ἀνδρός) Cyr. VII 5, 8
ἑστηκώς.

ἐπί c. Gen. = Proximity.

ποταμοῦ An. II 5, 18 ὧν. IV 3, 28. Hell. VII 4, 29. [1. Hd. Th.
X. 6]

6.—ORATORY.

ἐπί c. Dat. = Superposition.

ἀτυχήμασι Din. 1, 29 ἐπιγεγραμμένον.
γόνασι Lys. 18, 10 κατέθηκεν. [X. 6]
γραμματεῖον Dem. 45, 18 ᾧ, γεγρά-
φθαι.
ἐλπίδι [Dem.] 17 ἠκόνησαν . . .
θυμούς.

ἐπιγράμματι Isae. 5, 38.
ἑστίαις Dem. Frg. 17. [3. 4]
ἐσχατιᾷ Dem. 42, 5 ὅρος ἔπεστιν.
Cf. §§9, 26, 28 χρέως ἐ. τῇ ἐσχ.
[Cf. 1. Pl.]
θεμελίοις Hyper. 4, 6 οἰκοδομοῦσι.

μνήματι Dem. 44, 30 ἐφέστηκεν.
Alcid. Odys. 24 ἐπιγράμματα.
[X. Pl.]
νενεανιευμένοις (τοῖς) Dem. 21, 18
ἐπέθηκεν.
ὁδῷ (γήρως) Lyc. 40. Hyper. 1, 20.
ὁρίοις τοῦ βίου (*i. e. grave-stones*)
Lyc. 109.
πυρᾷ Aesch. 1, 146 (ὥς φησιν ὁ
ποιητής). [3. Hd.]
τάφῳ Dem. 44, 18 ἐφέστηκεν.
[Hd. 6]
τείχεσι Lyc. 47. [Th. X. τειχίων
4]

φιάλαις Dem. 22, 73 γέγραπται,
gen. in same §. 24, 181. [6]
ψήφισμα Aesch. 2, 68 ᾧ ἐπεγέ-
γραπτο.
Ἑρμῆς *statue of H.* Aesch. 3, 184
ἐπιγέγραπτο.
Ἡδυλείῳ Dem. 19, 148.
γυνή Aesch. 1, 183 ἐφ' ᾗ ἂν ἁλῷ
μοιχός.
δάμαρτι Lys. 1, 30 μοιχὸν λαβών.
Dem. 23, 55. Cf. also 59,
§§41, 65, 67, 72, 85, 86.

ἐπ' ἀκταῖς is found in an oracle supposed to be quoted by Aesch.
3, 112 and inserted in the text from Pausanias. Isoc. 17, 42
ὁλκάδα ἐφ' ᾗ χρήματ' ἦν ἐγὼ δεδωκώς[1] is of course graphic (see p. 8),
but if admitted to the list would make it difficult to exclude many
other instances only slightly less so. Dem. 58, 55 τοὺς ἐ. τοῖς
μακροῖς πλοίοις and many similar phrases, as also Din. 1, 62 ὁ ἐ. τῷ
ὀρύγματι and the like, are official, for which see Append. A, 2. ἐπὶ
δάμαρτι seems to be an old legal phrase, and though perhaps
weakened in the classical period, must have been literal originally.

ἐπί c. Dat. = Proximity.

δικαστηρίοις Lys. 30, 3. Isoc. 15,
38. Dem. 23, 63. [6]
ἐργαστηρίοις Isoc. 18, 9. [6]
θαλάττῃ Isoc. 4, 145, 163. Dem.
6, 12. 23, 78, 155. [Hd. Cf.
Pl.]
θύραις Lys. 3, 27, 29. 12, 16 -ᾳ.
Dem. 10, 34. 47, 37 -ᾳ. [Hd.
6]
μνήματι Dem. 47, 69. [X. 6. Pl.]
ὁδοῖς Aesch. 1, 124.
ποταμῷ Aesch. 3, 183.
στήλῃ And. 1, 38 ἐφ' ᾗ.

τάφῳ Lys. 2, 1 παρόντες, 60.
Hyper. 4, 1. [Hd. 6]
τραπέζῃ *bank* Lys. 9, 5. Isoc. 17,
2 -αις. 12, 44, 53 -αις. Dem.
19, 114 -αις. 27, 11 (2). 45,
33. 47, 57, 64. 48, 12. 49,
17, 42. 52, 24. [Pl. Cf. 1.
4. Hd.]
Ἀρτεμισίῳ Dem. 18, 208. 59, 95.
Aesch. 2, 75.
Δελφινίῳ Isae. 12, 9. Dem. 23, 74.
Δηλίῳ [And.] 4, 13.

[1] Prof. Gildersleeve conjectures δεδανεικώς, comparing Dem. 36, 6.

Εὐρίπῳ Lys. 24, 25.
Εὐρυμέδοντι Lyc. 72.
'Ιτόρι Dem. 13, 23. 23, 199.
Aesch. 3, 184.
Θρασύλλῳ Aesch. 1, 101. Schol.:
ἐ. Θρασ. δὲ ἀττικῶς ἀντὶ τοῦ πρὸς
τῷ Θρασύλλου μνήματι.
'Ιερῷ Dem. 20, 36. Schol.: τόπος
ἐστὶ περὶ τὸν Ἑλλήσποντον.
Κωλιάδι Dem. 59, 33.

Λαυρίῳ And. 1, 38.
Παλλαδίῳ Isoc. 18, 52. Dem. 23,
71. 47, 70. 59, 9. Aesch. 2,
87.
Παλληνίῳ And. 1, 106.
Πρυτανείῳ Dem. 23, 76.
Σουνίῳ Lys. 21, 5.
Τροίᾳ Dem. 19, 337.
Φυλῇ Lys. 12, 52. 13, 77, 79, 82.
Aesch. 3, 187.

ἐπί c. Gen. = Superposition.

ἀγκύρας Dem. 18, 281 ἐ. τῆς αὐτῆς
(sc. ἀγ.) ὁρμεῖ. 50, 22 ἀποσα-
λεύειν. 56, 44 -αιν, ὁρμεῖν.
ἀγρῶν Isoc. 7, 52.
ἀκτῆς Ant. 5, 44. [1. 2. 3]
ἀστράβης Lys. 24, 11, 12. Dem.
21, 133.
βάθρων Lys. 13, 37. [Hd.]
βήματος Ant. 6, 40. Lys. 10, 15.
Isoc. 5, 82, 129. 8, 54, 121.
12, 143. Isae. 5, 25. Dem.
6, 30. 7, 1. 12, 2, 19. 14, 41.
18, 312. 22, 68. 26, 19. 48,
31. 58, 40 ἐ. τῶν δικαστηρίων
καὶ τοῦ βήματος. Aesch. 1, 35.
2, 44. 3, 167, 257. [Demad.]
17.
βωμοῦ And. 1, 112. Lys. 2, 12
-ῶν. 6, 52 -ῶν. 13, 52. Isae.
Frg. 65 (= Teubner 14) -ῶν,
ἐτίθετο. Isoc. 6, 68. Dem. 7,
40 ἐπίγραμμα. [1. 2. 3. 4. Hd.
Th.]
γῆς Isoc. 4, 32. 10, 50 ἀλλοτρίας
(sc. γῆς). Dem. 19, 267 ἐφ'
ἧς. [1. 3. X. Pl.]
γονάτων [Aesch.] Epist. 4, 3.
[1. 4. X. 6]
διαθήκης Dem. 45, 21 ἐπῆν.

ἐσχάρας Dem. 59, 116. [1. 2. 3]
ζεύγους And. 1, 45. Dem. 21, 158.
ἠπείρου Isoc. 4, 35. 5, 112. 12,
44, 166.
ἵππος Isae. 11, 41 ἐφ' οὗ. Dem.
21, 174 ἀλλοτρίου. Aesch. 2,
111 -ου. [Aeschyl.]
κλίνης And. 1, 61. [Pl.]
κόρρης Hyper. Frg. 100. Dem.
21, 72, 147.
νεώς Lys. 21, 6, 8. Dem. 17, 27.
34, 2, 9, 12. 50, 54. 56, 7.
Aesch. 3. [52]. [Hm. 3. 4.
Th. X. Pl.]
ξένης Ant. 2, β 9 -ίας. Lys. 12,
98. Isoc. 4, 168. 19, 23.
Lyc. 25, 124. Dem. Epist. 3,
38.
οἰκίας Dem. 31, 3 ὅρους. [Pl.]
ὀνομάτων Aesch. 3, 253 πλεῖν as
on a ship.
προσώπου Hyper. Frg. 198 ἔπεστιν.
[1. 2. 4. Pl.]
σκηνῆς stage Dem. 19, 337.
τέγους Lys. 3, 11 κατέστασαν.
τριήρους Lys. 19, 24. Dem. 50,
52 ἐφ' ἧς.
τροχοῦ Ant. 5, 42. Hyper. 1, 39.
Dem. 29, 40.

35

φιαλῶν Dem. 22, 73 = 24, 181
γεγραμμένον. [6]
φορείου Din. 1, 36.
χωρίου Dem. 31, 3 ὅρους.
ὤμων Isoc. 19, 39. [1. 3]

'Ασίας Isoc. 12, 103.
Εὐρώπης Isoc. 4, 176. 5, 152.
Θράκης Isoc. 7, 9. 15, 108. Dem.
8, 64. 9, 26. 10, 65. 19, 219.
Aesch. 2, 9. 3, 73.

ἐπί c. Gen. = Proximity.

δικαστηρίου Isoc. 15, 49 -ων. Isae.
5, 1, 19, 25, 29. Frg. 4.
Hyper. 2, 2. Dem. 29, 16,
18. 48, 50. 58, 32, 40 -ων.
59, 66. Aesch. 1, 114. [6]
ἐργαστηρίων Isoc. 7, 15. Hyper.
3, 33 -ου.
θυρῶν Lyc. 40. [1. 2. 4. Hd. X.
6. Pl.]

ἰατρείου Aesch. 1, 40, 41, [50].
μνήματος Isae. 8, 27. [6. Pl.]
ποταμοῦ Dem. 18, 216. [1. Hd.
Th. X. 6]
τάφου [Dem.] 60, 30. [3. 6]
τομίων Dem. 23, 68 στάς.
'Εννεακρούνου Isoc. 15, 287 ψύχου-
σιν οἶνον.

As doubtful may be reckoned Dem. 59, 67 ἐπ' ἐργαστηρίου καθῶν-
ται (see Append. A, 6), Aesch. 1, 74 ἐ. τῶν οἰκημάτων καθεζομένου,
Din. 1, 23 ἐπ' οἰκήματος ἔστησεν, Dem. 34, 37 ἐ. τῆς στοᾶς. Problematic is Dem. 19, 156 τἀπὶ τειχῶν. For official designations, as ὁ ἐ.
τοῦ ὀρύγματος, see Append. A, 2.

7.—PHILOSOPHY (Plato).

ἐπί c. Dat. = Superposition.

αὐχένι Symp. 189 e. Phaed. 89 b.
[3]
γένος Timae. 75 b τὸ τῶν ἀνθρώπων
γένος σαρκώδη ἔχον ἐφ' ἑαυτῷ . . .
κεφαλήν.
γῇ Phaed. 111 a ἐπ' αὐτῇ (Bodl.
Hermann, Schanz; but Bek-
ker, Stallbaum, Wagner,
Wohlrab read αὐτῆς). Minos
317 d. Epist. 7, 335 b. [1.
2. 3. 4. Th. X. 6. Pl.]
κεφαλῇ Symp. 212 e. Rep. 600 d
-αῖς. [4. Hd. X. Pl.]
κλίναις Protag. 315 d παρεκάθητο.
[4. Hd. 6. Pl.]

κώλοις Timae. 76 e (ἄκροις).
μνήμασι Laws 933 b. [X. 6]
ναῦς Laches 183 d ἐφ' ᾗ ἐπεβάτευεν.
[1. 2. 3. 4. Hd. Th. X. 6]
νώτῳ Phaedr. 247 b. [Hd. Th.]
ὄρεσι Phaed. 116 e. [3. 4. Hd. X.]
οὐδῷ (γήραος) Rep. 328 e.
προσώποις Symp. 190 a. [1. 4. 6]
πυρᾷ Rep. 614 b. 621 b. [3. Hd.]
σώματι Timae. 90 a ἄκρῳ.
ἄλλῳ
ἑκάστῳ } Parmen. 131 b, c.
πολλοῖς

ἐπί c. Dat. = *Proximity.*

θαλάττῃ Rep. 404 c. [Hd. Pl.]
θύραις Symp. 183 a. 203 d. Laws
  933 b. [Hd. 6]
ὁδῷ Hipparch. 229 a.
οἰκίᾳ Symp. 174 d. [6]
πηγαῖς Critias 111 d. [1]
τραπέζαις *banks* Hipp. Min. 368 b.
  [Pl. Cf. 1. 4. Hd.]

τριόδοις Laws 933 b.

Ἀρτεμισίῳ Menex 241 a.
Δηλίῳ Apol. 28 e.
Εὐρυμέδοντι Menex 241 e.
Ληναίῳ Protag. 327 d.

ἐπί c. Gen. = *Superposition.*

ἀγρῶν Laws 637 a.
ἀλογίας Phileb. 14 a σωζοίμεθα as
  on a raft.
ἁρμάτων Lys. 208 a ἐ. τινος τῶν ἁρμ.
  Critias 116 e -ος. [3]
ἀσπαλάθων Rep. 616 a.
βάθρων Protag. 315 c. 325 e.
  [Hd.]
γεφυρῶν Critias 116 a ἐπιστήσαντες.
γῆς Symp. 195 e. Menex 246 d.
  Gorg. 523 e. Laws 906 b.
  Phaed. 109 c ἄνω. 110 b. 114 c.
  Timae. 22 c. d. 43 e. 44 d.
  59 d. e (2). 80 a. 92 a. Laws
  728 a. [1. 3. X. Pl.]
δελφίνων Critias 116 e.
ἐλπίδος Laws 699 b ὀχούμενοι.
ἐσχατιᾶς Laws 842 e. [1. 2. 6]
θαλάττης Phaed. 109 c *on surface*
  of. [Cf. Hd. Th. X. 6. Pl.]
ἵππων Menon 93 d. Laws 789 d.
  Symp. 221 a -ου. Rep. 467 e.
  Περὶ Ἀρετῆς 377 b. [Aeschylus]
κεφαλῆς Symp. 212 e. Rep. 617 c
  -ῶν. [Hd. X. Pl.]
κλινῶν Rep. 372 d κατακεῖσθαι.
  [Pl.]
κολλόπων Rep. 531 b.
κόρρης Gorg. 486 c. 508 d (2).
  527 a.

κρανίων Symp. 195 e.
κρηπῖδος Laws 736 c. [X.]
κύκλων Rep. 617 b (2) ἄνωθεν, and
  ἐφ' ἑκάστου.
μαλθακοῦ Symp. 195 e.
μέσου Parmen. 138 c. d.
μηχανῆς Clitoph. 407 a.
ξενίας Cratyl. 429 e.
ξύλον Rep. 479 c ἐφ' οὗ.
ὀμφαλοῦ Rep. 427 c καθήμενος. [3]
ὀχήματος Phaed. 85 d. 113 d τούτων.
πλευρᾶς Rep. 388 a quoting Il.
  24, 10. [4]
ποδός Polit. 270 a.
προσκεφαλαίου Rep. 328 c.
ῥοπᾶς Locr. Timae. 97 e. Cf.
  Th. V 103, 2.
σκελοῖν Symp. 190 d (2, σκέλους).
σκληροῦ Symp. 195 e.
σμικροῦ Timae. 62 b.
στιβάδων Rep. 372 b.
σχεδίας Phaed. 85 d. [X.]
τροχοῦ Euthyd. 294 e.
χαμαιζήλου Phaed. 89 b (2).
ὤμων Rep. 613 c. [1. 3]

ἀλλήλων Theaet. 195 a. [1. 3. 4.
  Th.]

ἐπί c. Gen. = Proximity.

τραπεζῶν banks Apol. 17 c. [6. Pl. Cf. 4.]

Doubtful again is ἐπ' οἰκήματος καθημένῳ Charm. 163 b, see Append. A, 6.

SUMMARY.[1]

	Dative.		Genitive.	
	Superposition.	Proximity.	Superposition.	Proximity.
Homer,	223	121	138	9
Hes. and Hy.	61	11	28	0
Lyric,	40	22	29	0 (or 1 ?)
Tragedy,	105	37	97	0
Aristoph.	24	25	65	0
Com. Frgs.	13	5	22	1 (?)
Herodot.	33	68	95	6
Thucyd.	19	56	80	2
Xenoph.	46	58	142	3
Orators,	31	65	65	24
Plato,	22	13	71	1
	617	481	834	46

Such then is the evidence offered by the remains of Greek literature down to the time of Aristotle. Simple inspection of this evidence closes the first point of the inquiry at once. *The dative case with ἐπί was certainly used in Attic speech to express simple superposition.* Of course exceptions may be taken to the lists, many of the rulings may seem arbitrary in the matter of admissions and exclusions, many cases may be explained away on the score of phraseology and quotation, as ἐπὶ δάμαρτι, ἐπὶ γήρως ὁδῷ, and others. But excluding these and ruling out of the Attic court the evidence of Thucydides and Xenophon, as Mr. Rutherford does, there still remain too many datives to be ignored in comedy, in the orators, and in Plato, free respectively from all suspicion of parody, Sicilian flavor, and poetic flight.

And yet in comparing the words of the Homeric list with the lists of the historians, orators and Plato, we feel that the atmosphere has changed. Objects are not so concrete, and, in the

[1] The table shows the whole number of instances given in the lists, but does not include those words mentioned in the notes as of doubtful classification, hence does not represent the whole local usage.

classic period, there is a sort of unreality about many of the
datives of superposition. Although their number reads fairly
high, we cannot help feeling that it would not be right to say τὸν
πῖλον ἔχων ἐπὶ τῇ κεφαλῇ. Nor could the Greeks have regarded the
cases as a matter of indifference, else their use of the dative would
have more nearly approached in number that of the genitive.
Their feeling may have been a vague one—one perhaps for which
they could have assigned no reason. But since an acquirement
of the feeling for these almost insensible distinctions is the ultimate essential to a complete appreciation of any language, and
since the search for these more delicate distinctions is not consid-
ered hopeless, e. g. between ἀνά and κατά,[1] between the imperf. and
aor., between subjunc. and optat., so in the present matter we
shall not lose hope, but take up in

PART II.

The Difference between ἐπί c. Gen. and ἐπί c. Dat.

Denoting Superposition.

A brief examination of the distinctions set forth by the authorities above quoted will suffice to show how unclear and untenable
they are.

Whether or not Kühner's distinction for Xen. An. 7, 4, 4 was
intended for general application is not clear, as it does not stand
at the head of its paragraph. Nor is the remark itself clear, for
wherein the horses or Alcibiades' head could exhibit a " Thätigkeit" is not obvious. And yet dimly as Kühner has uttered it,
there may be a grain of truth in his words, for which see p. 46.

By no possible mental strain can Krüger's distinction be applied
even to any single list, much less carried through the language.
We soon find that the use of the gen. to express "eine mehr
zufällige freiere Verbindung" is itself *zufällig*, while to connect
the notion of "Zugehörigkeit" with the dat. rather than with the
gen. is to do violence to all the ordinary associations of both
cases. How for instance can the notion of *Zugehörigkeit* be suggested by the dat. in ἔτι ἥλιον εἶναι ἐ. τοῖς ὄρεσι Phaed. 116 e, πορε-
κάθηντο δὲ αὐτῷ ἐ. ταῖς πλησίον κλίναις Protag. 315 d, ἐ. τῇ κεφαλῇ ἔχων

[1] For the distinction between ἀνά c. acc. and κατά c. acc. see J. B. Bury,
The Isthmian Odes of Pindar (1892), Append. H, founded on Hermann,
Opusc. V 41. See Keelhoff in Rev. de Philologie for 1892, p. 157.

τὰς ταινίας Symp. 212 e, ἐκεῖνον μὲν κατέθηκεν ἐ. τοῖς γόνασι τοῖς Παυσανίου
Lysias 18, 10, ἐ. δεκάμνῳ (sc. θώρακι) . . . καθήμενος Ar. Pax 1235?
Sobolewski also, p. 100, footnote, of the work cited above, says:
"ut *necessaria* est coniunctio rerum in Nub. 1176 et Av. 487, sic
fortuita in Lys. 1026, Thesm. 1182, aliis multis."

So far is Krüger's notion from giving satisfaction that Professor
Gildersleeve would "expect the natural position to be expressed
by ἐπί c. gen., the unnatural by the dat.," etc., see p. 6. This,
coupled with what he has said elsewhere (*Pindar*, Introductory
Essay, p. 99: "ἐπί is used most frequently with the dat., when
the superposition sense makes itself felt"), is the correct view, as
will be shown, it is hoped, later.

Mr. Monro's distinction seems only to echo Kühner's—"the
gen. usually with less definitely local force than the dat."—though
in clearer terms. Yet no reason is suggested *why* the gen. should
be used to designate the "great divisions of space, etc." Perhaps, however, this is well; for the rule goes no further than the
examples. Why, for instance, should it not apply as well to ἀκτή
and θίς as to ἀγροῦ? And why do not γαίη and χθών come under
the rule? And—which is yet more difficult—how reconcile the
rule with the fact stated in his Gram., §145, 2, that the locat. dat.
though "restricted to a comparatively narrow range," is also
especially used to designate these same "great divisions of the
world, the chief spheres of action, etc., as αἰθέρι, οὐρανῷ, οὔρεσι, ἀγρῷ,
αἰγιαλῷ, χέρσῳ"? Mr. Monro's second category for the gen.,
"where the local relation is a familiar one," is identical with Professor Gildersleeve's "natural position," and as stated above
points to the truth, although many examples contravene it, as
ἐπὶ γόνασι (κρατί, κλισμοῖσι, θρόνοισι, δίφρῳ, ἀπήνῃ), and its reconcile-
ment is not easy with the first distinction of the paragraph, viz.
that the gen. is less definitely local.

Giseke's theory I have reserved for the last, although histori-
cally earlier than some of the others. Presented originally in his
essay *Die allmähliche Entstehung der Gesänge der Ilias aus
Unterschieden im Gebrauch der Präpositionen nachgewiesen*,
Göttingen, 1853, it has appeared in a more enduring form in the
article on ἐπί in Ebeling's *Homeric Lexicon*, 1885. I therefore
give the theory the space which its prominent position claims.

Taking up the prep. ἐπί (p. 125) he says "dass in ἐπὶ νῆα
βαίνειν der Accus., seiner Natur nach, den Gegenstand bezeichnet,
welcher das leidende Ziel einer Thätigkeit, der Endpunkt einer

Bewegung ist; ἐ. νηὸς βαίνειν hingegen heisst 'das Schiff betreten,' und der Gen. drückt aus, dass derjenige, welcher vom Festlande aufs Schiff steigt, in einem andern Zustand übergeht. Die Sprache fasst das Local Schiff als die Ursache, welche diese Veränderung in dem Zustande des bewegten Gegenstandes hervorbringt und setzt, ohne Rücksicht auf die Richtung der Bewegung, den Gen. νηός, weil derselbe andeutet, dass von dem Schiff eine Wirkung ausgehe." Then quoting B 351–52 νηυσὶν ἐπ' ὠκυπόροισιν ἔβαινον | 'Αργεῖοι and translating the dative here by " auf, in Schiffen," he says : " Die Argeier und die Schiffe werden nicht als zwei getrennte Gegenstände angesehen, von denen der eine auf den andern wirkt (wei, beim Accus. ἐπὶ νῆα βαίνειν, die Vorstellung 'Schiff' sich ändert durch den neu hinzukommenden bewegten Gegenstand, wie, bei ἐπὶ νηὸς βαίνειν, der bewegte Gegenstand durch das Schiff verändert wird), sondern es werden beim Dat. beide Gegenstände als zu einander gehörig und verbunden gedacht." Proceeding to examples he finds that the gen. is used in κ 62 ἐπ' οὐδοῦ ἑζόμεσθα (of the suppliant Ulysses and his companions), η 169 ἐπὶ θρόνου εἶσε and other passages, "weil das Local auf den Zustand der Person wirkend[1] gedacht wird." " Fehlt aber die Veränderung des Zustandes, od. soll auf dieselbe kein Gewicht gelegt werden, so steht der Dat., wie bei den Freiern, bei denen es sich selbst verstand dass sie nicht auf der Schwelle sassen (ρ 90 ἐ. κλισμοῖσι κάθιζον), od. von den Ruderuden stets, z. B. β 419, ἐπὶ κληῖσι κάθιζον, denn es versteht sich von selbst dass sie sich auf die Ruderbänke setzten, und nicht anderswohin, wenn sie entschlossen waren abzufahren." After other illustrations he concludes (p. 128): " Daher kommt es dass der Gen. den Gegensatz ausdrücken kann dass etwas sich nicht auf diesem sondern auf einem eindern Gegenstande befindet; od. dass der Gen. den Ort mit besonderm Gewicht hervorhebt, während beim Dat. das Gewicht auf der Handlung liegt ἐ. κλισμοῖσι κάθιζον und ἐπ' οὐδοῦ ἑζόμεθα; dass endlich der Gen. dasjenige hervorheben kann was zufällig und gleichsam eine Ausnahme ist, während der Dat. die sich gleichbleibende Regel darstellt."

The first point in this conclusion is remarkable. ἐπί c. gen. tells us that an object is upon one thing and so by implication not upon another. Thus if we are told that a man is ἐπ' ἀγροῦ, the gen. bids us remember that he is not ἐν ἄστει. But does not the same

---

[1] But surely the time is past for finding the causal notion in all genitives.

implication exist in the case of the dat.? If a man be said to be
ἐ. νηί, we infer, with quite as much certainty as in the case of ἐπ'
ἀγροῦ, that he is not on land. Spinoza discovered long ago in
constructing his idea of an infinite God that *any* determination is
a limitation and involves the negation of its opposite. Any desig-
nation whatever therefore of the place discriminates against all
other places. It may be noted how diverse the impressions are
concerning the gen., for Giseke denoting the accidental and exceptional places, for Monro and Gildersleeve the familiar and
normal.

Giseke then proceeds to cite and comment upon further con-
firmatory passages, *e. g.* A 485–86 νῆα μὲν οἵ γε μέλαιναν ἐπ' ἠπείροιο
ἔρυσσαν | ὑψοῦ ἐπὶ ψαμάθοις, "denn das *Festland* verändert den
Zustand des Schiffes, der *Land* aber ist der Ort an dem es ruht";
ρ 357 κατέθηκεν | αὖθι, ποδῶν προπάροιθεν, ἀεικελίης ἐπὶ πήρης, "quia
mensa carebat" (in Ebeling's Lex.), and others.

It will be seen that Giseke firmly believes in the Causal Genitive. It is this belief which leads him into such (as they seem to
me) absurd explanations—perhaps nowhere more absurd than on
τ 470 τὸ δ' ἐπὶ χθονὸς ἐξέχυθ' ὕδωρ, where Eurycleia has recognized
Ulysses and has upset the basin. He says: "Wenn aber Eury-
kleia aus versehen die Badewanne umstösst und das zum Baden
bestimmte Wasser verschüttet, so ist der erste Gedanke dass das
Wasser sich verändere und hinfort nicht mehr zum Baden tauge;
deshalb heisst es ἐπὶ χθονός, denn der Erdboden macht in diesem
Falle das Wasser zum Waschen untauglich, und indem er es
somit in einen andern Zustand versetzt, wird er als auf anderes
einwirkend vorgestellt und steht im Gen." This passage, showing
the result to which Giseke's theory leads, is itself sufficient refutation of the theory.

Without further examination of opinions which all seem more
or less vaguely to hint at, but never to hit upon, the truth, which
lies at the basis of the distinction, the thesis of the present dissertation may be stated at once, viz.

The difference between ἐπί c. gen. and ἐπί c. dat. is a graphic
or pictorial difference, not a logical one; appealing to the fancy,
not to the reason. It is a difference of accent or of shading,
rather than of kind. Both give the place *upon which*, but ἐπί c.
gen. adds no separate item to the picture. It melts into it as a
subordinate element, necessary at times, but still subordinate.
Its presence may be felt, its absence noted, but it is a mere enclitic

42

in the thought. Whereas ἐπί c. dat. emphasizes the *place* of the object or action, presents it not as a background but as a second feature. Nor is the place an indefinite region, anywhere within which the object or action lies (for this is expressed by the gen.), but a definite point. There is no fusion here between the object and its environment. The iota of the original locative suffix -ι was as strongly deictic as the iota of οὑτοσί, pointing to this place here or that place there, and to no other. In the thought-accent the locative claimed an acute, and to this the Greek dat., its successor,[1] fell heir.

With the difference thus *based*, we see at once the reason of the facts noted by the scholars above quoted, as also the degree of truth which they severally reached. Why, for example, the gen. to express the familiar relations, the natural position? Evidently because no word-painting is aimed at. In the daily prose relations of life, the Greeks expressed plainly the necessities of the case, as we ourselves do, reserving emphatic expression for poetry and passion. Choosing the case therefore which most readily fuses with others, the one of such general affinities as to have no obtrusive individuality of its own, they spoke, *e. g.* of going ἐφ' ἵππου with no more thought of the personality of the horse than we when we speak of going 'on horseback.' The horse was a mere vehicle, the phrase well on its way to adverbial petrification (*cf.* ἔφιππος) and stood just as would βραδέως, ταχέως or any other adverb. But compare this with the manner in which Xenophon paints the picture of the exciting moment (Anab. I 8, 1) when Πατηγύας ... προφαίνεται ἐλαύνων ἀνὰ κράτος ἱδροῦντι τῷ ἵππῳ. The horse is no vehicle here. He stands out sharply, comitatively, as part of the picture.

Again, why is the gen. used when two objects are contrasted? Here surely the dat. if more emphatic would be more fitting. But it must be remembered that not the places of the objects are contrasted but the objects themselves, designated more exactly by mention of their localities. The gen. is still adjectival, as a means to an end. To illustrate from English—the merchant will speak of his 'New York establishment' or his 'Paris establishment,' but not of his 'establishment at New York,' which by presenting New York as a substantive rather than as an adjective

---

[1] Delbrück, *Synt. Forsch.* IV 130: "ἐπί mit dem Dativ ist natürlich nichts anderes als ἐπί mit dem Localis."

would lessen somewhat his establishment. Again we say: 'Your hat is on the table, not on the bed,' yet the table and bed, heavily as we stress them, are hardly within the conscious horizon of the picture. We know that you are seeking the hat, not them. Hence in Greek, with a proper accentuation of the thought, ὁ ἐ. τῆς τραπέζης (κλίνης) πῖλος.

It will be observed that the present distinction is the exact reverse of Giseke's. But let us see if it does not better account for the facts.

In the first place, it will be granted, I think, that the distinction which continues the same through the language has more in its favor than one which accounts for only one period of the language or in the course of time exactly reverses itself. Now by making the dat. the picturesque and emphatic means of indicating locality, the gen. the colorless means, we explain immediately poetic usage[1] and prose usage respectively (see the summary above), and also establish a distinction which runs through the language, varying in degree perhaps in the different departments and periods and traversed sometimes by the habits of the language, but still the same. Whereas Giseke's theory is on the horns of a dilemma. For, holding the dat. to be the unemphatic, the gen. the emphatic case, it *either* turns Homer and all succeeding poets into prose (Hm. with 223 datives against 138 genitives) and makes the Athenians talk poetry—without knowing it perhaps, as Mons. Jourdain talked prose—*or* it must admit and maintain that the language reversed its usage. Neither of these positions seems tenable.

Secondly, by distinguishing the cases as here proposed, we shall not run counter to all their other associations. For, as seen above in Delbrück's statement of the theory of preps. (p. 3), it is after all a question of the cases, not of prepositions.[2] Thus if we

---

[1] Tycho Mommsen, *Entwickelung einiger Gesetze für den Gebrauch der griech. Präpositionen*, p. 15: "Das Vorwalten des Dativs gehört der älteren und der poetischen Sprache."

[2] If this doctrine were applied in the school-grammars, cutting out the chapter on preps. and their illicit intercourse with the cases, and restoring the latter to their proper categories, the student might acquire the Greek feeling for the cases at an earlier age than is now usual. For example, what a cloud of misunderstanding rises from the boy's mind when first he *feels* that it is the same genitive case in αἰσθάνομαί τινος, μέμνημαί τινος, etc., as in τύπτομαι ὑπό τινος—the verb in this last instance being no more 'pass-

change οὗτος ὁ τοῦ τέγους 'you roof-man'[1] to οὗτος οὑπὶ τοῦ τέγους (Ar. Nub. 1502), instead of breaking up the relation between the two substantives we render it closer by clarifying it. Only the miserable custom of writing ὁ—ἐπὶ—τοῦ τέγους instead of ὁ ἐπιτουτέγους[2] has deceived us into thinking that there were three elements of thought in the phrase. There are two only. ἐπί has nothing to do with the case. The gen. would be chosen at any rate. And the two elements run so closely together, the one modifying the other, as expressed in English by the hyphen (roof-man), that only one image is presented, viz. the man-on-the-roof.[3] Again we easily feel in English the difference between 'I bought a five-dollar hat' and 'I bought a hat for five dollars.' In the former the hat is the sole object of vision, in the latter we are balancing two. In Greek the first instance would show the gen., the second the dat. or ἐπί c. dat.[4] For the dat. stands off. Whether person or thing (pure dat. or locat. dat.) it stands *there*, not here, either as an interested onlooker or as the place *towards* or *in* which. But there is hardly need of a reminder, much less of exposition, to show that all our associations with the two cases thus distin-

---

ive' than in the others. (Why indeed should a boy be required laboriously to acquire this *notion* of 'passivity,' when in later years he must again dissolve it and find that also even the *forms* of language expressing it are fictions?)

[1] Though Max Müller may have been wrong in supposing that formally the gen. was a genderless adjec., yet certainly its function and our feeling for it is adjectival.

[2] See, however, Paul, *Principien der Sprachgeschichte*, p. 278.

[3] We may compare this οὑπὶ τοῦ τέγους and the patronizing οὑπὶ κρεμάθρας ἀνήρ 'your basket-man' (Nub. 218) with the picturesque 'Charon at the oar' οὑπὶ κώπῃ ψυχοπομπός . . . Χάρων (Eur. Alces. 361).

[4] If it be objected that ἀντί c. gen. could also be used, it must be borne in mind that ἀντί is generally recognized as taking an adnominal gen., *i. e.* is almost an 'improper' prep. (See Monro, *Homeric Gram.*, §226.) The combination of a gen. with its noun or verb in presentation of a single idea is sometimes so close that no proportioning of the elemental notions seems possible. We cannot tell which is predominant. Thus in Κάστορος βίη the gen. is not merely a modification of the nom., for the succeeding construction is often masc., following the gen. So when a boy speaks of a 'whale of a ship' he is not thinking especially of a whale, nor on the other hand of a whaling-ship. Be the explanation of these gens. what it may—and it is certainly often wrong, as when Prof. Jebb thinks it may be a gen. of material in Soph. Ant. 114 λευκῆς χιόνος πτέρυγι στεγανός—the fact remains that the complex presents one image.

guish them. Against Giseke (who would contravene these associations) all that the present thesis recommends is this: Drop the
preposition and let the cases speak for themselves.

Thirdly, by thus making the distinction one of imagery and
representation rather than of logical coherence, we free ourselves
from the necessity of predicting with the book closed how an
author in any given case will prove to have expressed himself.
For, on a logical basis, things *must* be *so*, and not otherwise.
Hence the chains of argumentation which the logical Giseke
must throw about the Protean Homer to compel him to take on
a logical form. Hence, too, the widespread opinion among
schoolboys, painfully drilled into seeing and explaining the logical
basis of the various phenomena of the Greek language, that the
Greeks were the most illogical people in the world. Whereas,
regarded as imagery, all is plain, for all is subjectivity. Homer
in a given case felt the locality as a mere background and used
his brush in the gen. We, if the same case be given us, may feel
the need of more color in the scene, and prefer the dat. Both are
right, as subjectivity justifies itself.

But on examination of the lists, subjectivity will not often be
called upon to justify itself. In proportion to the whole number
of examples the number will be small where we should expect a
different case-usage, or where recourse need be had to a vaulting
fancy before reaching the author's point of view. Due allowance
of course must be made for the individual. Xenophon, for
example, may become flowery, as sometimes other soldiers or
travellers (one may compare Stanley's lectures and books on
Africa). But the broad distinction is this: Where there is painting in detail, where the march of thought is leisurely, or where
on the other hand there is excitement or pathos—the mind dart·
ing and insistent—there we expect the dat. Where there is but
one image to present, all else being subordinated, there we look
for the gen.

One further point must be disposed of before applying the distinction to the lists. The phraseology and habits of the language
cannot be ignored. They will at times, though rarely, seem to
traverse the rule that has been proposed. Yet on examination
they will bear good evidence to its truth. The first item, phraseology, enters the question very slightly. ἐπ' ἀγροῦ (-ῶν), for
example, runs through the language (including Apoll. Rhod. and
Theocr.), never with modifier and only four times with article.

ἐπὶ τῶν ἀγρῶν. The dat. is not used. The phrase is in fact one word, as much so as ἐπιδέξιος, though lacking declension. But there are only twenty instances in all. So a few other fixed phrases, as ἐπὶ θύραις (but with exceptions), ἐπὶ γήρως ὁδῷ, ἐπὶ δάμαρτι, ἐπὶ θινί (ῥηγμῖνι, χέρσου, ἠπείρου). But few of them are frequent, and most of them emerge only in certain departments or periods. Beyond this, phraseology does not disturb the question. χθών, γῆ, ὅρος, ἀκτή, αἰγιαλός and others change with the picture to be presented.

The second item, the habits of the language, may be instanced by the way in which the notion of a vehicle *upon which* is expressed, viz. by the gen. This, I think, is the one grain of truth which Kühner was struggling after above (p. 5) when he spoke of the ' Thätigkeit' of the horses, although the example to be sure was an unhappy one. In the above lists the following words occur literally or metaphorically as the names of vehicles, always in the gen. except the underscored words, which are sometimes dat., but in that case for the most part not as vehicles. *Waggons :* ἀπήνη. ἄμαξα, ἅρμα, ἁρμάμαξα, ἡμίονοι *mule-car,* ζεῦγος, ὄχος, ὄχημα, κάναθρον. Add κλίνη, φορεῖον, ἀστράβη, ἐφίππιον, κεφαλή. *Ships :* ναῦς, τριήρης, πλοῖον, ὁλκάς, δόρυ, σχεδία, διφθέρα, τεῦχος, ῥίψ, ῥοπή, ῥώμη, ἐλπίς, μάθημα, ἀλογία, ὀνόματα. *Beasts of burden :* ἵππος, ἱππάριον, κέλης, πῶλος, ὄνος, κάμηλος, στροῦθος, κάνθαρος, δελφίς, τρόπις.

On examining the passages where the underscored words appear in the dat., it will be seen that in the following cases at least the objects are not regarded as vehicles for the action expressed by the verb. ζ 75 ἐσθῆτα ... κατέθηκεν ... ἐπ' ἀπήνῃ. Aesch. Prom. 710 πεδάρσιοι ναίουσ' ἐπ' εὐκύκλοις ὄχοις (where the surprising nature of the habitation requires the dat.) Hm. Hy. 5, 19 ἁρπάξας ... ἐπὶ χρυσέοισιν ὄχοισιν is corrupt; see the list. Plat. Protag. 315 *d* παρεκάθηντο δὲ αὐτῷ ἐπὶ ταῖς πλησίον κλίναις (a Defregger interior, where κλίνη is of course not used as a litter, as in Andoc. 1, 61. Dem. 17, 20 (τριήρεις) καὶ στρατηγὸν ἐπ' αὐταῖς ἐτάξατε Μενεσθέα—an official dat., see App. A, 2. Dem. 58, 55 τοὺς στρατηγοὺς καὶ τοὺς ἐπὶ τοῖς μακροῖς πλοίοις—official. Ψ 362 ἐφ' ἵπποιῖν μάστιγας ἄειραν. ο 182 ἐφ' ἵπποιῖν μάστιν βάλεν. Aesch. Frg. 38 ἵπποι δ' ἐφ' ἵπποις ἦσαν ἐμπεφυρμένοι. μ 425 ἑζόμενος δ' ἐπὶ τοῖς (*sc.* τρόπιδι and ἱστῷ) φερόμην ὀλοοῖς ἀνέμοισιν—where the caesura indicates the proper connection of τοῖς with ἑζόμενος. For κεφαλῇ see p. 52. Β 351 νηυσὶν ἐπ' ὠκυπόροισιν ἔβαινον is a disputed reading, ἐν being preferred

by La Roche, Nauck, Christ, Faesi, and others. Ο 388 ξυστοῖσι,
τά ρά σφ' ἐπὶ νηυσὶν ἔκειτο. β 414 πάντα φέροντες εὐσσέλμῳ ἐπὶ νηὶ
κάτθεσαν. ω 419 τοὺς δέ ... θοῆς ἐπὶ νηυσὶ τιθέντες. Soph. Phil.
891 οὐπὶ νηΐ ... πόνος. Eur. Iph. T. 1109 ἐπὶ ναυσὶν ἔβαν—where
the ἐπί is Elmsley's, as the MSS. have ἐνί and ἐν. Thuc. IV 10, 4
ἐπὶ γὰρ ταῖς ναυσὶ ῥᾷστοί εἰσιν ἀμύνεσθαι—locality merely, or at any
rate with no notion of a vehicle. Xen. Hell. IV 3, 12 ἐπὶ τῇ νηὶ
μαχόμενον ἀποθανεῖν—locality. Plat. Laches 183 d (ναῦς) ἐφ' ᾖ ἐπεβάτευεν—official. Hermipp. Frg. 63, 11 ἐξολέσειεν ναυσὶν ἐπί—not
as a vehicle.

In the remaining six instances (four in poetry, two in prose) we
might expect the notion of a vehicle, but can by no means be
sure that such a notion was intended to be conveyed, especially
as the notion of pure locality or of instrument is quite as satisfactory. It is worthy of remark that the four poetical passages
came from Euripides, viz. Phoen. 1110 σφάγι' ἔχων ἐφ' ἅρματι ὁ μάντις
Ἀμφιάραος, Troad. 569 λεύσσεις τήνδ' Ἀνδρομάχην ξενικοῖς ἐπ' ὄχοις
πορθμευομένην—both passages highly picturesque, the chariot being
the first object to strike the sight, like Xenophon's sweating
horse—, Rhes. 236 Φθιάδων δ' ἵππων ποτ' ἐπ' ἄντυγι βαίη—which may
be corrupt, as two MSS., followed by Paley, Matthiae and others,
read ἄντυγα, and yet may stand with the other instances as an
example of Euripides' exaggerated poetical style—, Helen 1135
νεφέλαν (i. e. Helen) ἐπὶ ναυσὶν ἄγων—here clearly a case of the dat.
as vehicle. The only two examples in prose are: Xen. An. II
4, 28 οἱ βάρβαροι διῆγον ἐπὶ σχεδίαις διφθερίναις ἄρτους, τυρούς κτλ. and
Thuc. IV 67, 3 ἀκάτιον ἀμφηρικὸν ὡς λῃσταί, ἐκ πολλοῦ τεθεραπευκότες τὴν
ἄνοιξιν τῶν πυλῶν, εἰώθεσαν ἐπὶ ἁμάξῃ, πείθοντες τὸν ἄρχοντα, διὰ τῆς τάφρου
(lege κατὰ τὴν τάφρον) κατακομίζειν τῆς νυκτὸς ἐπὶ τὴν θάλασσαν καὶ ἐκπλεῖν.
The fact that these authors write exceptional Attic would perhaps
for many be sufficient explanation of this syntax. But the instances are worth attention. Xenophon's point was, not merely
that the barbarians got food across the river, but that they used a
novel mode of conveyance, hence (besides διφθερίναις) the dat. of
instrument, to which ἐπί is almost adverbial. The Thucydidean
passage is still more instructive. The long periodic sentence,
with its circumstantial detail, would almost compel the use of the
dat. ἐπὶ ἁμάξης preceding the verb at such a distance would be
flat. Thucydides may have lived long away from Athens, may
have been perverse in style, used archaic spelling, poetic words
and harsh hiatus, but here surely he wrote as any cultured Athe-
nian would write, sensitive to thought-accent.

48

It is clear therefore that this particular habit of the language, the expression of the vehicle by the gen., was very strictly observed, there being but two exceptions in prose and three (or four) in Eurip., all five being easily accounted for by the fact that the object was something more than a vehicle in the picture which the author was presenting.

Thus much, by way of instances, for the phraseology and habits of the language. We now turn to the lists to apply the distinction maintained. But as it will be impossible within the limits of this essay to examine all the examples, let us first look at those of single instance—the οἰωνοί of the language—in the hope that here too their solitariness (according to the ancient derivation of the word) may prove prophetic. We shall begin at the end of the lists, as Attic Greek is the special object of the search.

1) τραπεζῶν (= *banks*).—Plat. Apol. 17 c λόγοι) δι᾽ ὧνπερ εἴωθα λέγειν καὶ ἐν ἀγορᾷ ἐπὶ τῶν τραπεζῶν, ἵνα ὑμῶν πολλοὶ ἀκηκόασι, καὶ ἄλλοθι, a solitary instance of ἐπὶ τραπεζῶν in the sense of banks, for not only Lys., Isoc. and Dem. use the dat., but also Plato himself, Hipp. Min. 368 b ὡς ἐγώ ποτέ σου ἤκουον μεγαλαυχουμένου, πολλὴν σοφίαν καὶ ζηλωτὴν σαυτοῦ διεξιόντος ἐν ἀγορᾷ ἐπὶ ταῖς τραπέζαις —. And yet the difference is clear. The former passage is colloquial. to be sure, and circumstantial, yet melting into one thought, unconscious, making no point of the locality. The Hippias passage, on the contrary, is sarcastic, there are pauses between the clauses, each word tells, and a slight emphasis on the locality is not without significance in the case of the money-making sophist. In Lys., Isoc. and Dem. the dat. is of course in place, as in all business transactions dates and places must be carefully designated.

2) ἀλλήλων.—Plat. Theaet. 195 a ἐὰν δὲ πρὸς πᾶσι τούτοις ἐπ᾽ ἀλλήλων συμπεπτωκότα ᾖ ὑπὸ στενοχωρίας. Elsewhere always ἐπ᾽ ἀλλήλοις, as would be expected, the very purpose of the word being to evoke two objects, and in the phrase ἐπ᾽ ἀλλήλοις to set one upon the other. But just here it is not Plato's purpose to call up two objects, but their *mixture*. The things are ὑγρά, the context tells us, and they have melted. ἐπ᾽ ἀλλήλοις would be positively wrong.

3) ἰσθμοῦ.—Thuc. I 13, 5 οἰκοῦντες γὰρ τὴν πόλιν οἱ Κορίνθιοι ἐπὶ τοῦ ἰσθμοῦ ἀεὶ δή ποτε ἐμπόριον εἶχον —. Thuc. I 56, 2 ὑποτοπήσαντες τὴν ἔχθραν αὐτῶν (sc. τῶν Κορινθίων) οἱ Ἀθηναῖοι Ποτιδαιάτας, οἳ οἰκοῦσιν ἐπὶ τῷ ἰσθμῷ τῆς Παλλήνης, Κορινθίων ἀποίκους, ἑαυτῶν δὲ ξυμμάχους φόρου ὑποτε-

λεῖς, ἐκέλευον —. These passages Kuemmell cites as proof of the indifference of the cases. To me no two passages could better prove the difference. In 13, 5 the thought-accent lies on ἀεὶ δή ποτε ἐμπόριον εἶχον, as is shown by what follows, while the participial clause is wholly subordinate. In 56, 2 the Potidaeans, their locality, origin, political status, are circumstantially presented, ἰσθμῷ has a gen. with it, all points are itemized. In our own language we draw hundreds of just such distinctions, unaware of their existence until some unlucky foreigner fails to observe them.

4) αὐχένων.—The next case of single instance is Aesch. Pers. 191, where Atossa is relating her dream. Xerxes yokes the two women

$$\text{ἅρμασιν δ' ὑπο}$$
$$\text{ζεύγνυσιν αὐτὼ καὶ λέπαδν' ἐπ' αὐχένων | τίθησι.}$$

Would not the ἐνάργεια of the dream be better served here by the dat.? Perhaps so; only there would then be too much ἐνάργεια. The women already fill the picture, with Xerxes, the yoking and the collar. Mention of the part of the body is incidental, emphasis upon it would be ludicrous, evoking the question: Where else, pray, if not on the neck?

5) κρηνάων.—Hes. Op. 757-8

$$\text{μηδέ ποτ' ἐν προχοῇ ποταμῶν ἅλαδε προρεόντων,}$$
$$\text{μηδ' ἐπὶ κρηνάων οὐρεῖν.}$$

Here ἐπὶ κρηνάων must mean *immediately over*, just as occasionally ἐπὶ ποταμοῦ, ἐπὶ θαλάσσης are used, for which see p. 53.

6) πηγαί.—X 153 of the fountains

$$\text{ἔνθα δ' ἐπ' αὐτάων πλυνοὶ εὐρέες ἐγγὺς ἔασιν.}$$

The fountains had been already described. The πλυνοί are now taken up, the fountains serving as a mere point of reference. We too, we accent '*near* them,' not 'near *them.*' Compare this with the very different effect of the datives in the Catalogue, where the homes of the various contingents are most carefully set forth, *e. g.* B 523 οἵ τε Λίλαιον ἔχον, πηγῇς ἔπι Κηφισοῖο. So too the careful dat. in locating the palace of the great king, Xen. An. I 2, 8 ἐν Κελαιναῖς ἐρυμνὰ ἐπὶ ταῖς πηγαῖς τοῦ Μαρσύου ποταμοῦ ὑπὸ τῇ ἀκροπόλει, and in marking the place of the κρήνη ἡδέος ὕδατος καὶ ἄφθονος ῥέουσι ἐπ' αὐτῇ τῇ θαλάσσῃ ὑπὸ τῇ ἐπικρατείᾳ τοῦ χωρίου (An. VI 4, 4).

This completes the list of words which depart in only one instance from the habits of the language. Before proceeding to those of greater variation, a second habit of the language may here be stated once for all, to which the last example from Homer, ἐπ' αὐτάων, has led us, viz. the unemphatic pronoun αὐτοῦ decidedly prefers the unemphatic gen. case, there being in post-Homeric Greek sixteen instances of ἐπ' αὐτοῦ to five of ἐπ' αὐτῷ, or, if cases of superposition alone be reckoned,[1] to only one ἐπ' αὐτῷ. This solitary instance of αὐτῷ to denote superposition (Xen. Cyr. VI 1, 54) is worth inspection. Cyrus builds a portable tower and stations men upon it καὶ πολὺ ῥᾷον ἦγε τὰ ὀκτὼ ζεύγη τὸν πύργον καὶ τοὺς ἐπ' αὐτῷ ἄνδρας ἢ κτλ. The graphic ἐπ' αὐτῷ is not 'upon it,' but 'perched on top of it,' men and tower, two objects. The rule, however, requires the gen., as the figures 16 to 1 certainly show, although the unusual nature of the event would at times cause us to expect the dat. So, e. g. Hd. 6, 129 ὁ Ἱπποκλείδης . . . ἐκέλευσέ οἱ τινα τράπεζαν ἐσενεῖκαι, ἐσελθούσης δὲ τῆς τραπέζης πρῶτα μὲν ἐπ' αὐτῆς ὠρχήσατο Λακωνικὰ σχημάτια. But altogether too strong would be in English too: "he ordered a table to be brought and when brought danced upon it (αὐτῇ).

This habit of αὐτοῦ (wholly in accord with the non-emphatic character of the gen. as here claimed) effectually dispels Kuemmell's difficulty in distinguishing Thuc. IV 100, 4 φλόγα ἐποίει μεγάλην καὶ ἦψε τοῦ τείχους, ὥστε μηδένα ἐπ' αὐτοῦ ἔτι μεῖναι from VIII 69, 1 ἦσαν Ἀθηναῖοι πάντες ἀεί, οἱ μὲν ἐπὶ τείχει, οἱ δ' ἐν τάξει, . . . ἐφ' ὅπλοις, on which he says in despair "ne minime quidem interesse sentio."

The same habit would also seem to establish a seventeenth instance of the gen., viz. ἐπ' αὐτῆς (sc. γῆς), Plat. Phaed. 111 a, as Bekker, Stallbaum, Wagner, Wohlrab have, rather than ἐπ' αὐτῇ as the Bodl. MSS., Hermann, and Schanz read. The reference to the preceding γῆ is a wholly unemphatic one.

Returning to the lists we next take up

7) γονάτων.—There are only two instances of ἐπὶ γονάτων. [Aeschin.] Epist. 4, 3 describing the statue of Pindar πρὸ τῆς βασιλείου στοᾶς, καθήμενος ἐνδύματι καὶ λύρᾳ ὁ Πίνδαρος, διάδημα ἔχων καὶ ἐπὶ τῶν

[1] Thuc. uses ἐπ' αὐτῷ twice, Herod. once, of proxim. to a river, Herod. ἐπ' αὐτῇ once of proxim. to an island.

γονάτων ἀνειλιγμένον βιβλίον. Xen. Conv. 9, 4 ἐπεί γε μὴν κατεῖδεν αὐτὴν (sc. 'Αριάδνην) ὁ Διόνυσος, ἐπιχορεύσας ὥσπερ ἃν εἴ τις φιλικώτατα ἐκαθέζετο ἐπὶ τῶν γονάτων. In the former case Pindar has two things, a wreath and an open book, the place of the book being designated incidentally, but furnishing no third item in Pindar's make-up. Dionysus in the Xenophon passage dances up to Ariadne and seats himself upon her lap—not a remote or surprising place for the lover, as the dat. would have represented it. In the instances of ἐπὶ γόνασι either the verbs more naturally take a dat., as κατέθηκεν (Lysias), θεῖναι, καθίσσας (Hm.), καθιζομένη (Ar. Thesm. 1182—where it is not for love, however, as with Dionysus and Ariadne), or there is pathos and the etching is deep. X 500 Andromache lamenting Hector from the walls and telling of Astyanax, ὃς πρὶν μὲν ἑοῦ ἐπὶ γούνασι πατρὸς | μυελὸν οἶον ἔδεσκε. Xen. Cyr. VII 3, 5 τὴν δὲ γυναῖκα λέγουσιν ὡς κάθηται χαμαὶ κεκοσμηκυῖα υἷς εἶχε τὸν ἄνδρα (her slain husband), τὴν κεφαλὴν αὐτοῦ ἔχουσα ἐπὶ τοῖς γόνασι.

8) θυρέων, -ῶν.—In place of ἐπὶ θύραις, the regular phrase in frequent use from Hm. down, ἐπὶ θυρέων (-ῶν) occurs three times: Hdt. 3, 120. 5, 92 γ. Lycurg. contra Leocr. 40. I confess here to seeing no reason whatever for the departure from usage. In the Herodotean passages one is almost led to suspect corruption of the text, some one of Herodotus' late admirers substituting by slip the phrase of his own times. For that the use of ἐπί c. gen. to denote proximity became more common—though never extensive—in later times is seen by reference to Polybius (see Krebs, *Die Praepos. bei Polyb.*, 1882) and to the New Testament. Lycurgus' break with the habitual phrase is the more possible, or rather probable, as already in his time ἐπί c. gen. had lost its earlier stability of signification and showed various metaphoric uses and connections with abstracts. Why not, therefore, also in connection with concretes show development? Besides, in his desire to increase the tensity of his expression (already throughout quite tense enough), he may have seized on the less emphatic gen. because unusual, and by this contravention of the usual attained the emphasis aimed at.[1] Or can it literally mean (ὁρᾶν

---

[1] This method of obtaining an effect (viz. by reversal of the natural means) may be seen in any art which has reached its full growth. In modern music, for example, love scenes and the *andante* movement of the symphony are often given *fortissimo*, the *finale* on the contrary *pianissimo*.

δ' ἦν ἐπὶ μὲν τῶν θυρῶν γυναῖκας ἐλευθέρας περιφόβους κατεπτηχυίας) that the timid women pressed cowering upon the doors?

9) κεφαλή.— In Plato's Sympos. 212 e (too long for quotation) stands first a description of Alcibiades standing at the door ταινίας ἔχοντα ἐπὶ τῆς κεφαλῆς πάνυ πολλάς, and within the same paragraph he says νῦν δὲ ἥκω ἐπὶ τῇ κεφαλῇ ἔχων τὰς ταινίας. "Absolutely no difference," say some. And yet see how delicately and perfectly Jowett has given the difference. Alcibiades "appears at the door . . . his head flowing with ribands," and then says "I am here to-day carrying on my head these ribands." The change in the order of Greek words points to just this difference in thought-accent, ταινίας claiming attention in the first, ἐπὶ τῇ κεφαλῇ in the second passage, as Alcibiades proves by his next clause, ἵνα ἀπὸ τῆς ἐμῆς κεφαλῆς τὴν τοῦ σοφωτάτου καὶ καλλίστου κεφαλὴν ἀναδήσω. Compare again the change of cases and the change of position, effecting the same change of thought-accent as here, in Rep. 600 d καὶ ἐπὶ ταύτῃ τῇ σοφίᾳ οὕτω σφόδρα φιλοῦνται, ὥστε μόνον οὐκ ἐπὶ ταῖς κεφαλαῖς περιφέρουσιν αὐτοὺς οἱ ἑταῖροι and 617 c Μοίρας, λευχειμο-νεύσας, στέμματα ἐπὶ τῶν κεφαλῶν ἐχούσας.

In Hdt. 5, 12 σκευάσαντες τὴν ἀδελφεὴν ὡς εἶχον ἄριστα, ἐπ' ὕδωρ ἔπεμπον ἄγγος ἐπὶ τῇ κεφαλῇ ἔχουσαν καὶ ἐκ τοῦ βραχίονος ἵππον ἐπέλκουσαν καὶ κλώθουσαν λίνον, while in the last sentence of the same chapter the same woman appears φέρουσα τὸ ὕδωρ ἐπὶ τῆς κεφαλῆς καὶ ἐπέλκουσα ἐκ τοῦ βραχίονος τὸν ἵππον καὶ στρέφουσα τὸν ἄτρακτον. "Here again no difference," say some. "The gen. and dat. are as undistinguish-able here in function as in the dual they are in form." But the true explanation is this: Herodotus having once painted the picture in detail, has no further need of the itemizing dat. Like a good artist, he chooses for the repetition the more summary and incidental gen., at the same time shifting it, as Plato did, into the less prominent position after the verb.[1] In his minutely-detailed account of the dress of the various tribes under Xerxes, Herodotus invariably uses, when describing their head-gear, ἐπὶ τῇσι κεφαλῇσι, as might be expected (VII 70, 72, 74, 75, 76, 79, 84), the dat. preceding the verb in every instance but once—one other

---

[1] This same lightening of the touch on repetition is seen in Eur. Hec., where in v. 698 the slave-woman tells of the dead Polydorus ἐπ' ἀκταῖς νιν κυρῶ θαλασσίαις full of the horror of the scene, while in v. 778 the grim Hecuba, still self-restrained before Agamemnon, responds to his question as to the finder ᾐδ', ἐντυχοῦσα ποντίας ἀκτῆς ἐπι. See also Herod. III 28 ἐ. μὲν τῷ μετώπῳ . . . ἐ. δὲ τοῦ νώτου.

instance lacking its verb. Xenophon also uses the dat. in describing head-gear (An. V 4, 13. VII 4, 4); further, in an instructive instance of the attributive position, where the attributes are themselves contrasted, and do not, as is usually the case, stand subordinate and in the gen., viz. An. II 5, 23 τὴν μὲν γὰρ ἐπὶ τῇ κεφαλῇ τιάραν βασιλεῖ μόνῳ ἔξεστιν ὀρθὴν ἔχειν, τὴν δ' ἐπὶ τῇ καρδίᾳ ἴσως ἂν ὑμῶν παρόντων καὶ ἔτερος εὐπετῶς ἔχοι.

10) ποταμοῦ, θαλάσσης.—Proximity to water is regularly expressed by ἐπί c. dat. But Xenophon three times, and Demosthenes once, has ἐπὶ ποταμοῦ, Herodotus once ἐπὶ θαλάσσης and once ἐπ' αὐτοῦ (sc. Βοσπόρου). The distinction is clear. The gen. presents the object as immediately over the water, its image reflected in and one with it ; the dat. denotes proximity merely, but the water remains a distinct object. In Xenophon's first passage ἐπὶ ποταμοῦ is literally upon, An. II 5, 18 ποταμοί) ἐφ' ὧν ἔξεστιν ἡμῖν ταμιεύεσθαι ὁπόσοις ἂν ὑμῶν βουλώμεθα μάχεσθαι (i. e. over the fords of the rivers). So too in the second, An. IV 3, 28 ἰδὼν δὲ αὐτοὺς διαβαίνοντας Ξενοφῶν πέμψας ἄγγελον κελεύει αὐτοῦ μεῖναι ἐπὶ τοῦ ποταμοῦ μὴ διαβάντες—they were therefore actually in or on the river, not somewhere in the neighborhood, as ἐπὶ τῷ ποταμῷ might mean. His third gen., Hell. VII 4, 29 ἐπὶ δὲ τοῦ Κλαδάου ποταμοῦ παρετάξαντο must mean, as in Hesiod's ἐπὶ κρηνάων, 'on the very brink of,' as the seat of the Olympian games could have offered only close quarters for a battle. Dem. 18, 216 δίς τε συμπαραταξάμενοι τὰς πρώτας, τήν τ' ἐπὶ ποταμοῦ καὶ τὴν χειμερινήν is of doubtful historical reference and must be passed over or else taken as an instance of the crumbling of Greek idiom already alluded to. Of the two Herodotean passages, one shows the pronoun of reference and is properly in the gen. (see above, p. 50), θεησάμενος δὲ καὶ τὸν Βόσπορον στήλας ἔστησε δύο ἐπ' αὐτοῦ λίθου λευκοῦ (IV 87), while in the other (III 5) ἀπὸ ταύτης (sc. Καδύτιος πόλιος) τὰ ἐμπόρια τὰ ἐπὶ θαλάσσης μέχρι Ἰηνύσου πόλιος ἐστι τοῦ Ἀραβίου, Herodotus is mapping out the land and uses the sea as an adjective (the sea-ports). The gen., consequently, is the only proper case.

We turn next to those cases in Aristophanes which to Sobolewski prove the indifference of gen. and dat. He compares Eq. 752 ff.

> ὁ γὰρ γέρων
> οἴκοι μὲν ἀνδρῶν ἐστι δεξιώτατος,
> ὅταν δ' ἐπὶ ταυτησὶ καθῆται τῆς πέτρας,
> κέχηνεν κτλ

with Eq. 783 σὲ γὰρ . . . .

> ἐπὶ ταῖσι πέτραις οὐ φροντίζει σκληρῶς σε καθήμενον οὕτως
> οὐχ ὥσπερ ἐγὼ ῥαψάμενός σοι τουτὶ φέρω. ἀλλ' ἐπαναίρω
> κᾆτα καθίζου μαλακῶς κτλ.

From all that has been said, the distinction here must strike
every one. In the first passage there is a contrast of Demos at
home with Demos at the pnyx. The places are used attributively
(*this* Demos and *that* Demos), and in themselves are of no
importance. But in the second passage how pathetic are those
hard rocks—real rocks that hurt you when you sit upon them,
not the pnyx rock of the other occasion where men voted and
clamored. " I have bought a cushion which I made for you.
Now you can sit softly on those hard rocks." Evidently the
sausage-seller makes the πέτραι all-prominent. The difference
between the two passages so far from being *nil*, is enormous.
Sobolewski again holds up Vesp. 1040 ἠπίαλοι καὶ πυρετοί)

> οἳ τοὺς πατέρας τ' ἦγχον νύκτωρ καὶ τοὺς πάππους ἀπέπνιγον,
> κατακλινόμενοι τ' ἐπὶ[1] ταῖς κοίταις ἐπὶ τοῖσιν ἀπράγμοσιν ὑμῶν
> ἀντωμοσίας καὶ προσκλήσεις καὶ μαρτυρίας συνεκόλλων κτλ.

in comparison with Lys. 575 πρῶτον μὲν ἐχρῆν, ὥσπερ πόκον ἐν βαλανείῳ

> ἐκπλύναντας τὴν οἰσπώτην, ἐκ τῆς πόλεως ἐπὶ κλίνης
> ἐκραβδίζειν τοὺς μοχθηρούς κτλ.

and Lys. 732

> ἀλλ' ἥξω ταχέως νὴ τὼ θεώ,
> ὅσον διαπετάσασ' ἐπὶ τῆς κλίνης μόνον.

But the difference here is no less than before. Note the personi-
fication and high imagery of the first passage—the murderous
Ἠπίαλοι and Πυρετοί strangling old men and scheming in the night-
watches—a passage direct from *Les Misérables*. Whereas in
Lys. 575 what object does ἐπί κλίνης serve ? Merely to make plain
the metaphor, nothing more. As for Lys. 732, the woman does
well not to emphasize the κλίνη by using the dat. See the schol.:
διαπετάσασα τὰ ἔρια, εἰς τὸ κακέμφατον δὲ αἰνίττεται.

Sobolewski does not study the context. He fails to see that
syntax can no more be understood bit by bit than a mosaic. He
has not grasped the fact that syntax is, if not the man, at all

---

[1] Hamaker reads ἐν.

events, the occasion. Lucian writing did fairly well as an Atticist, but Lucian embarrassed was shocked to find what errors he was capable of. Carlyle when in a passion went back to his mother-Scotch. The nerves of an organized sentence can be slack or tense just as the muscles of the human body. Its tone is discovered by a careful diagnosis of just such symptoms as ἐπί τινος, ἐπί τινι. Ignoring such symptoms, we run the risk of the Greek becoming truly a dead language for us.

Without devoting further space to particular instances, it may be well to inquire what relation this distinction bears to the developed uses of ἐπί c. gen. and ἐπί c. dat. Can they be deduced from it and so bear witness to it, or not? On even a cursory glance it will be seen that they do. Taking the meanings at random, first, of ἐπί c. dat.: to eat (drink) one thing with another (ἐπί τινε) presents the image of two objects, not one, and the gen. is impossible (see p. 59). So in the official phrases (p. 60) where the wagons, camels, machines, ships claim our thought more than the man in charge of them, while the official gen. on the contrary sinks these things in the personality of the officer. οὑπί τοῦ ὀρύγματος, for example, was perhaps as concrete an individuality as the modern Beefeater. So the various actions and occasions at which one may be present (ἐπ' ἀγῶσι, συμβολαίοις, διαθήκῃ, δείπνῳ, etc.) So, temporally, to do one thing after another, and in the phrases ἐπὶ τούτῳ, ἐπὶ τῷ τρίτῳ σημείῳ, φόνος ἐπὶ φόνῳ, ἄχθος ἐπ' ἄχθει, etc. So to post one next to another τάττειν (καταστῆσαι) τινὰ ἐπί τινι, to follow on another ἕπεσθαι ἐπί τινι, the rearguard οἱ ἐπὶ πᾶσι. So Eur. Alc. 373 μὴ γαμεῖν ἄλλην τινὰ γυναῖκ' ἐφ' ἡμῖν. So the hostile ἐπί in μηχανᾶσθαι (τεκταίνεσθαι, συνομνύναι, τάττειν, μάχεσθαι) ἐπί τινι. So the ἐπί of price, calling up two objects and their exchange, while the gen. subordinates the price to the thing purchased. So the further extension of ἐπί to denote condition, cause, purpose. Throughout the whole list two objects are presented.

ἐπί c. gen. on the contrary becomes phraseological, fuses, and presents a composite, whose elements are not easy to disengage, by themselves not making obvious sense. From the time of Homer's εὔχεσθε ... σιγῇ ἐφ' ὑμείων (H 195) 'pray in silence to yourselves,' there is something subjective about it, the image returning to itself, no second object allowed to intrude.¹ So in

¹ See Krüger's Xen. An. V 4, 34 for the difference between γελᾶν ἐφ' ἑαυτοῦ and γελᾶν ἐφ' ἑαυτῷ.

the military phrases ἐπὶ φάλαγγος (κέρως, ἑνός, τριάκοντα, ὀλίγων) ἄγειν, τάττειν, γίγνεσθαι, etc. So even in the ἐπί of direction (ἐπὶ Σάμου πλεῖν), where the gen. is the "characteristic of the motion" and goes as immediately with its verb as the word *west* in our phrase 'to go west.'[1] In all cases the gen. presents an object which melts at once into the chief object of the thought or serves as a mark by which it may be recognized. The developed uses therefore of ἐπί c. gen. and ἐπί c. dat. favor the distinction maintained.

A second support may be found in the behavior of the sister preposition ὑπό. Why does it prefer the dat. in its local sense? (That it does so may be seen by reference to Appendix C.) Evidently for this reason. If one thing be *upon* another, we see it without effort, there is nothing to call forth remark, and, on ordinary occasions, we would use the gen. ἐπί τινος. But the being *under* a thing does not strike us as a natural (normal) position. Things under other things are apt to be hidden and to be passed over, as proved by ἐπί 1455 times against ὑπό 345 times (not including Plato entire or the lyric fragments). But if we do see things under other things, their situation cannot but impress us. And what case can better draw attention to locality than the dative? Hence ὑπό·τινι, just as ἐπί τινι, to emphasize the place.

A third point in favor of the theory that the distinction between the gen. and dat. with ἐπί must be based in imagery and not in logic is the remarkable difference of construction shown by certain verbs, *e. g.* by βάλλειν and ἰέναι. The latter prefers the gen., βάλλειν and ἐπιβάλλειν the dat. or accus., never perhaps in all classic Greek taking the gen. They are not found with the gen.

---

[1] Definition of the cases may as well be abandoned. If the nearest definition of the accus. is : "eine Ergänzung oder nähere Bestimmung des Verbalbegriffs," then countless genitives are accusatives. For, as said above, the dispute as to whether it is the verbal element in a noun or the nominal element in a verb which attracts the gen. seems sheer logomachy, particularly supererogatory in the case of the Greeks, who cudgelled their brains many a century before discovering (or fancying they had discovered) the difference between a noun and a verb. Query : did the Greeks lack discernment here or is it we, warped by early training into seeing distinctions where none exist? Yet at last we may be floating back to the definitionless open sea of the Greeks. See Professor Gildersleeve, *Johns Hopkins Un. Circulars* for 1883, p. 67 : "The adjec. is a ptc. at rest, the ptc. is an adjec. in motion. A similar difference is seen between the abstract noun and the infinitive." But if rest and motion are relative, then verb and noun are one.

in Homer,[1] Hesiod, Pindar,[2] Aeschylus, Sophocles, Aristophanes, Herodotus, Thucydides, Xenophon, Plato,[3] or Theocritus. All editors are dissatisfied with Sappho 102 ἦρ' ἔτι παρθενίας ἐπιβάλλομαι, and Eur. Orest. 51 has been rejected as an interpolation, while γουνάτων in Eur. Suppl. 272 goes of course with ἀντίασον, and ἐσχάρας in Cycl. 384 is accus., thus leaving as the solitary example in classic Greek[4] of βάλλειν with the gen. Eur. Suppl. 286 τί κλαίεις λέπτ' ἐπ' ὀμμάτων φάρη | βαλοῦσα τῶν σῶν;[5] Why this difference of construction in verbs of the same signification? Clearly because of the mental image evoked by them. With βάλλω our eyes follow the missile to its goal, while ἱέναι simply lets it fly.[6] ἱέναι therefore chooses the subjective case, βάλλω the objective. But if verbs elect their construction by reference to the imagery of the cases, why may not also prepositions?

It would be an additional acceptable support to the theory if the use of modifiers and of the definite article gave evidence for it. For on first thought we might expect that the case which tended to phraseological formations would seldom show modification, or, if any, that it too would be of the stereotyped sort; also that the article would be more frequently lacking than with the livelier dative. Now, though the figures do not run counter to this surmise, yet the difference between the number of modified genitives and modified datives is not great (28 *per cent.* of the genitives to 36 *per cent.* of the datives). And on second thought we could not expect it to be otherwise; for stereotyped phrases and brevity of phrase are just as necessary when speaking of two

---

[1] Z 68 ἐνάρων ἐπιβαλλόμενος is the nearest approach, but the verb is here in the middle voice, *the thrower is the missile.*

[2] Ol. I 58 κεφαλᾶς βαλεῖν is 'from the head.'

[3] Sisyphus [Plato] 391 *a* does indeed show τὸν πλειστάκις βάλλοντα τοῦ σκοποῦ, but Sisyphus is not Plato's.

[4] The following examples of βάλλειν c. gen. are quoted in N. T. lexicons : βεβλημένον, -ην, ἐπὶ κλίνης Mt. 9, 2, Mk. 7, 30 (which hardly count, as βάλλω is in the perfect). ἐὰν ἄνθρωπος βάλῃ τὸν σπόρον ἐπὶ τῆς γῆς Mk. 4, 26. βαλοῦσα γὰρ αὕτη τὸ μύρον τοῦτο ἐπὶ τοῦ σώματός μου Mt. 26, 12.

[5] If the gen. be allowed here, however, to the introspective and erratic Euripides, ἐσχάρας may be gen. in Supp. 272.

[6] See Schmidt, *Synonymik der Griechischen Sprache* III, §104, p. 151 : " βάλλειν unterscheidet sich so von ῥίπτειν und ἱέναι, dass die Erreichung des Orts-Objekts dabei direkt ins Auge gefasst wird." Page 155: "Endlich ist auch hervorzuheben, dass mit ἱέναι nicht einmal notwendig die Trennung von dem Subjekte angegeben wird. Od. 6, 231. Il. 19, 383. 22, 316."

58

objects as when speaking of one, if not more so. For example, we speak of the man ἐπ' αὐτοφώρῳ (without the article) briefly, yet clearly see culprit *and* crime, while the phrase οὑπὶ τοῦ ὀρύγματος (with the article) calls up but one image—the hangman's. Here, therefore, there is no evidence either for or against the distinction maintained.

I am well aware that the principle of *repraesentatio* here claimed must, if true, be of much greater extension than the present essay has set forth. A picturesque use of the cases would hardly confine its exhibition to a connection with two prepositions (ἐπί and ὑπό). But certainly there is nothing in the nature of the two cases to render such a distinction improbable. On the contrary many points have been presented in its favor.[1] If *repraesentatio* has been found so potent in the moods of indirect discourse, why not also in the cases? Its images may sometimes appear illogical, and logic be compelled to retire baffled. But if analogy is admitted to have played many pranks with logic, why may not *repraesentatio* do so? Reason is not yet dominant in language. Thanks to imagery, the sun still ' rises.' Without absolute revolt, therefore, from logic and statistics, we may do well at times (especially if we have statistics with us) to go back to Dionysius of Halicarnassus and judge the phenomena of language by ἄλογος αἴσθησις, or at any rate to avoid the Charybdis of ἀναίσθητος λόγος.

[1] Other small points may be pointed out, *e. g.* that vv. of action prefer περί c. acc., vv. of thought and speech περί c. gen. For the difference between διά c. gen. and διά c. acc. I quote Gildersleeve, *Introductory Essay to Pindar*, p. 98 : " With the gen. the passage is already made, or as good as made. In Pyth. 9, 133 παρθένον ἀγεν ἱππευτᾶν Νομάδων δι' ὅμιλον, we may imagine elbowing, but it may be imagination." But it is more than that.

APPENDICES.

A.

Excluded Instances of ἐπί.

A necessary complement to the lists presented in this essay is a list of exclusions, the heads of which will be here given. The question what to omit and what to include has been by no means always an easy one, and the decision will often perhaps seem arbitrary. For while in this special inquiry the guiding principle is apparently simple, viz. that of the concreteness of an object, or, in the case of metaphors, the vividness of the image presented, yet just what the vivid image is and just what metaphor has become so remote as to be dead are questions which can be correctly answered only as one approximates to Greek thought and feeling. Neither logic nor the analogies of our own language should be allowed to influence the decision. Yet I think such has been the case in the first of the following heads:

1. It seems to be the common opinion that in such phrases as ἐσθίειν ἐπὶ τῷ σίτῳ ὄψον (Xen. Mem. III 14, 2), κάρδαμον ἔχειν ἐπὶ τῷ σίτῳ (Cyrop. I 2, 11), ἐπί c. dat. is not purely local but means 'in addition to' or 'with.' In deference to this opinion I have omitted such phrases from the lists. Yet if our own phrases had been 'bread *on* meat' and 'butter *on* bread' instead of what they are, perhaps the purely local notion would have been more readily allowed to the Greek. This error of classifying the phenomena of a language by the translations made from it into one's own is an old one, against which Rumpel raised a warning voice in his *Casuslehre*, p. 80. The following is a complete list of such exclusions:

ἁλί Ar. Ach. 835 παίειν . . . μάδδαν.

ἀλφίτοις Ar. Plut. 628 μεμυστιλη-μένοι.

ἀμβροσία Pl. Phaedr. 247 e ἐπ' αὐτῇ νέκταρ ἐπότισεν.

βαλλαντίῳ Ar. Eq. 707 φάγοις . . . ἄν.

κολλύρα Ar. Pax 123 ἕξετε . . . ὄψον ἐπ' αὐτῇ.

λάχανα Aristophon 13, 8 (II) πίνουσιν ἐπὶ τούτοις ὕδωρ.

σίτῳ Xen. Cyrop. I 2, 11 κάρδαμον

. . . ἔχωσιν. VI 2, 27 πίνειν ὕδωρ.

Mem. III 14, 2 ἐσθίουσι . . . ὄψον.

ταρίχει Ar. Ach. 967 λόφους κραδαινέτω. Ar. Frg. 630 γέλωτα κατέδομαι. Chiondes 6 (I) κόπτετον (?).

τρίγλη Antiph. 26, 11 (II) κατεσθίει γοῦν ἐπὶ μιᾷ τὴν οὐσίαν.

ψωμῷ Xen. Mem. III 14, 5 ὄψων γεύεσθαι.

In this connection Homer frequently has the adverbial ἐπὶ δέ *thereupon, therewith*, and Blaydes has made a collection of passages on Ar. Plut. 1005, where ἐπεσθίειν also takes the dative.

2. Another wide use of ἐπί c. dat. is to designate the things or persons, over which one has been appointed officer, overseer, or the like; also the post at which one is stationed. Here the local meaning does not suffice or has altogether disappeared. Attention has been already called to some of the earlier instances, as *e. g.* Homer's ἐπὶ βουσί. The following is of course not a complete list:

καταλιπεῖν τινα φύλακας ἐπί — Xen. Cyrop. IV 5, 15. ἐπὶ τῷ πυρί Anab. IV 2, 14. ἐπὶ τοῖς ὑποζυγίοις καὶ ὀχήμασι Cyrop. V 3, 34. ἐπὶ ταῖς ναυσί Hellen. I 5, 11.

αἱρεῖσθαι ἐπὶ τοῖς παισί (ἐφήβοις, τελείοις ἀνδράσι) Cyrop. I 2, 5.

τάττειν ἐπὶ τριήρεσι Dem. 17, 20. ἐπὶ ταῖς τιμωρίαις Isoc. 5, 117. ἐπὶ τῇ κοινῇ φυλακῇ Dem. 17, 15. See also Dein. 1, 112. Dem. 60, 22. Aesch. 2, 73.

ἐφεστάναι ἐπί — Isoc. 3, 48, and many other verbs.

Also with the article ὁ (οἱ) ἐπὶ ταῖς μηχαναῖς Xen. Cyrop. VI 3, 27. ἐπὶ ταῖς καμήλοις Cyrop. VI 3, 33. ἐπὶ τοῖς ἄλλοις ἅρμασι Cyrop. VI 3, 36. ἐπὶ τῷ ὀρύγματι Dein. 1, 62. τοῖς πράγμασι Dem. 8, 76. 9, 2 ὄντες. ἐπὶ τοῖς ξένοις . . . ἐγένετο Dein. 1, 74.

Here must be catalogued, and not elsewhere, such instances as the following: ἀλλ', εἰ βούλει, μέν' ἐπὶ τῷ στρατεύματι Xen. Anab. III 4, 41. τοὺς στρατηγοὺς καὶ τοὺς ἐπὶ τοῖς μακροῖς πλοίοις Dem. 58, 55. παρῆσαν αἱ . . . νῆες . . . καὶ ἐπ' αὐταῖς ναύαρχος Πυθαγόρας Xen. Anab. I 4, 2. Κνῆμον μὲν ναύαρχον ἔτι ὄντα (καὶ τοὺς ὁπλίτας) ἐπὶ ναυσὶν ὀλίγαις εὐθὺς πέμπουσι Thuc. II 80, 2. This last passage gives trouble to Kuemmell, but the fact is that the local has vanished before the official usage, and Captain Knemos is sent *with* or *in command of* a few ships. As a test, let one try to satisfy himself with the purely local notion, and he will see that the image presented is uncalled for by the context, and absurd. On the other hand, if the notion of conveyance had been intended, the whole usage of the language, where no emphasis is present, would have demanded the genitive. Kuemmell may as well revert to the purely local notion of ὑπό in Thuc. IV 44, 4 οὐ κατάδηλος ἡ μάχη ἦν ὑπὸ τοῦ ὄρους.

Examples of the official genitive are: οἱ ἐπὶ τῶν ὁπλιτῶν Lys. 32, 5. ὁ ἐπὶ τοῦ ὀρύγματος Lycurg. 121. τοὺς ἐπὶ τῆς πολιτείας ἐφεστηκότας

Dem. 19, 298. τοὺς ἐπὶ τῶν πραγμάτων Dem. 18, 247. Dem. Proem. 30, 1. ἐπὶ τῶν πράξεων Dem. Proem. 55, 3. τὸν ἐπὶ τῶν ὑπηρετικῶν Aeschin. 2, 73. τοὺς ἐπὶ τούτων ἐπεστεῶτας Herod. 4, 84; etc. For the difference between these and the dat. see p. 55.

3. A third more difficult and indeed impossible line to draw was that which should separate the local ἐπί and the more vivid of the temporal ἐπί's from the gradually less vivid temporal use which finally loses all imagery in *e. g.* (τὰ) ἐπὶ τούτοις (τῷδε). Beginning, therefore, with η 120 ὄγχνη ἐπ' ὄγχνῃ and Ξ 130 ἐφ' ἕλκεϊ ἕλκος, I have excluded all those instances which involved any notion of time (φόνον ἐπὶ φόνῳ, πάθος ἐπὶ πάθει, etc.), even though the local image was strong.

4. Again, in the honors to the dead shown *over* the corpse at the tomb or elsewhere, the step is easy from the local to the derived meaning, and to distinguish them is sometimes difficult. One may compare P 706 ἐπὶ Πατρόκλῳ ἥρωι βεβήκει, where the sense seems merely local, with Π 661 πολέες γὰρ ἐπ' αὐτῷ κάππεσον and with Ψ 776 βοῶν) οὓς ἐπὶ Πατρόκλῳ πέφνεν . . . Ἀχιλλεύς, where ἐπί is often translated 'in honor of.' Compare also Xen. Anab. I 8, 29 οἱ μέν φασι βασιλέα κελεῦσαί τιν' ἐπισφάξαι αὐτὸν Κύρῳ (said to be local) with Cyrop. VII 3, 7, where the same phrase ἐπισφάττειν τινί is said to mean 'in his honor.' In accordance with custom, I have therefore ruled out the following and like instances, though in many the local sense seems sufficient: Xen. Hellen. III 2, 5 θάψαντες τοῖς ἑαυτῶν καὶ πολὺν οἶνον ἐκπίοντες ἐπ' αὐτοῖς. Aesch. Ag. 1547 τίς δ' ἐπι-τύμβιος αἶνον ἐπ' ἀνδρὶ θείῳ . . . πονήσει; Aesch. Eum. 329 ἐπὶ δὲ τῷ τεθυμένῳ τόδε μέλος. Eur. Alces. 148 οὔκουν ἐπ' αὐτῇ πράσσεται τὰ πρόσφορα; Herod. VII 225 ὁ λίθινος λέων ἕστηκε ἐπὶ Λεωνίδῃ. And the frequent phrase λέγειν ἐπί τινι of epitaphios orations, *e. g.* Thuc. II 34, 6 and 8. 35, 1. Lysias 2, 1 and 2. Isoc. 4, 74. Dem. 18, 285. 60, 1.

5. It seemed best also sharply to cut off many abstracts, though giving such clear evidence as they do to the usage of the language in the original concretes. And so, though θύραις is admitted, I have excluded 1) προθύροις, ἐξόδοις, εἰσόδῳ, ἐσβολῇ, ὑρίοις, ὅροις, ἐσχάτῳ, ἀρχῇ, ὁρμῇ, τέρματι, τέλει, τελευτῇ; also (though sometimes admitting χώρα) τόπῳ, -οις, -ον, στρατοπέδῳ, φρουρᾷ, κέρᾳ, ὅπλοις *camp*, etc. 2) (though admitting δικαστηρίοις) ἀγῶσι, δίκῃ, διαίτῃ, μαρτυρίαις, συν-θήκαις, and other phrases of occasion such as ἐπὶ δείπνῳ, συναικλίαις, etc. The following is a complete list of words (and their refer-ences) of the character of those under 1):

ἀρχῇ Theognis 607. Plat. Timae. 48 d.

διαβάσει (of a river) Thuc. VII 78, 3. Xen. An. VI 3, 5. Hell. VII 2, 10. Mag. Eq. 4, 5 (pl.).

δυσμαῖς Xen. An. VII 3, 34.

ἐσβολῇ Thuc. IV 83, 2.

εἰσόδῳ Xen. Cyr. I 3, 11.

ἐμβολῇ Xen. Hell. IV 3, 10. 7, 7 (pl.).

ἐξόδοις Aesch. Sept. 33. 58. Eur. Hel. 1165. Ion 575. Rhes. 514. Xen. Hell. V 4, 4 (ἐξόδῳ τῆς ἀρχῆς).

ἐσχάτῳ Plat. Charm. 155 c. Protag. 344 a. Rep. 523 e.

εὐναῖς (camp) Thuc. VI 67, 1.

εὐπροσοδωτάταις Xen. Hell. VI 5, 24.

κέρᾳ (of army, either right or left) Hd. 9, 102. Thuc. I 49, 6. II 90, 2. IV 43, 4 ἐφ' ᾧ. 93, 4. 94, 1. V 67, 1 (2). VI 67, 2. 101, 4. Xen. An. I 8, 20. VI 5, 11. Hell. III 2, 15 (2). IV 4, 9. V 2, 40, 41. Oec. 4, 19.

Λυδαῖς Soph. Trach. 356.

λουτροῖσι Soph. Elec. 445.

μέσῳ (of army, like κέρας) Xen. An. VI 5, 11.

ὅπλοις camp Com. Frg. Adesp. 663 (III). Thuc. VII 28, 2. VIII 69, 2. Xen. Cyr. VII 2, 8.

ὁρίοις Thuc. II 12, 3. Xen. An. V 4, 2. Cyr. II 4, 31. VIII 5, 21. Hell. VII 2, 1. 4, 39.

Andoc. 1, 45. Lycurg. 47. Dem. 18, 174, 230.

ὁρμῇ Plat. Timae. 27 c.

ὅρμῳ Thuc. III 76, 1.

ὅροις Aesch. Prom. 666. Eur. Med. 540. Hd. (οὔροισι) 3, 91. 5, 52. Xen. Hell. VII 2, 20.

οὐρᾷ (of column of men) Xen. Hell. IV 3, 4.

προθύροισ(ι) Σ 496. a 103. Plat. Com. 4, 2 (II) (Bergk ἐπί, legebatur ἐνί). Eur. Alces. 101. Plat. Phileb. 64 c.

πρυμνοῖς (ἀγορᾶς) Pind. Pyth. V 93.

σκοπαῖς Xen. Cyr. VI 3, 6.

στενῷ Xen. Hell. VI 4, 3, 27.

στρατεύματι Isae. 4, 26.

στρατοπέδῳ Xen. An. VII 3, 1.

τελευτῇ Xen. Mem. I 5, 2 τοῦ βίου. Aeschin. 3, 205 τῆς ἀπολογίας. Plat. Gorg. 516 a τοῦ βίου.

τέλει Plat. Euthyd. 291 b, of a discussion. Menex 234 a. Leg. 730 c. 818 a. Polit. 268 d. Rep. 506 d. 532 b ἐπ' αὐτῷ γίγνεται τῷ τοῦ νοητοῦ τέλει ὥσπερ ἐκεῖνος τότε ἐπὶ τῷ τοῦ ὁρατοῦ.

τέρματι, -σι Aesch. Eum. 633. Eur. Heracl. 278. Charmus (perh. See Bergk, II, p. 379). Hd. 7, 54. Xen. De Rep. Lac. 10, 1 τοῦ βίου.

τόπῳ, -οις Soph. Trach. 1100. Xen. Cyr. VIII 6, 17. Isoc. 5, 120.

ὑπερβολῇ Xen. An. IV 6, 6 (2), 24.

φρουρᾷ Dem. 54, 3 (Blass ἐν).

ψυχῇ Soph. Ant. 317.

63

Instances of the genitive case are the following:

καρτερῶν Thuc. III 18, 5.
κέρατος Hd. 9, 47. Xen. An. I
  8, 9. Hell. II 4, 13. VII 5, 25.
ὅπλων *camp* Xen. De Rep. Lac.
  12, 7.
πλευρῶν (of column of men) Xen.
  An. III 2, 36.
προαστείου Thuc. II 34, 5.

σκοπῆς Xen. Cyr. VI 3, 12.
στρατοπέδου Xen. An. VI 5, 4.
  Plat. Leg. 674 a.
τελευτῆς (τοῦ λόγου) Aeschin. 3,
  257.
τόπου Dem. 10, 23.
φρουρᾶς Xen. De Rep. Lac. 13,
  1, 11.

Here too, it appears, is there an oscillation between gen. and dat., but it is not a vacillation. The context will show that the dat. is deictic, the gen. adjectival—a difference strikingly shown by the two following passages: Dein. 3, 8 ἐπὶ μὲν τῶν ἄλλων ἀδικημάτων σκεψαμένους ἀκριβῶς δεῖ μεθ' ἡσυχίας καὶ τἀληθὲς ἐξετάσαντας, οὕτως πιτιθέναι τοῖς ἠδικηκόσι τὴν τιμωρίαν, ἐπὶ δὲ ταῖς φανεραῖς καὶ παρὰ πάντων ὡμολογημέναις προδοσίαις κτλ. Isoc. 15, 20 καὶ γὰρ αἰσχρὸν ἐπὶ μὲν τῶν ἄλλων πραγμάτων ἐλεημονεστάτους ὁμολογεῖσθαι . . . , ἐπὶ δὲ τοῖς ἀγῶσι τοῖς ἐνθάδε γιγνομένοις τἀναντία τῇ δόξῃ ταύτῃ φαίνεσθαι πράττοντας. It will be seen that secondary matters (ἄλλα) are disposed of with the genitive, important matters emphasized by the dative (note τοῖς ἐνθάδε γιγνομένοις in the last example).

6. Finally, the phrase ἐπ' οἰκήματος (ἐργαστηρίου, τέγους) has been excluded, when signifying places of prostitution. The passages are: Hd. 2, 121 ε, 126. Dem. 59, 67 ἐργαστήριον, by euphemism. Aeschin. 1, 74. Dein. 1, 23. Plat. Charm. 163 b. In view of the fact that Grecian houses were built low—perhaps especially the case with cheap houses of prostitution, mere slaves' quarters—Professor Gildersleeve has suggested as somewhat more than probable that the women literally sat upon them, just as other wares would be exposed to view.[1] See his note on ἐπὶ τέγους, Justin Martyr Apol. I 26, 15. One would be inclined to connect ἐπ' ἐργαστηρίων *workshops* thus immediately with the literal sense of ἐπί. But whether ἐπὶ δικαστηρίου (see the orators) should also be so treated is doubtful, in view of the rather extended use of ἐπί c. gen. in the sense of *coram*. One passage, however, certainly favors the literalness of the phrase, viz. Dem. 58, 40 ἐπὶ τῶν δικαστηρίων καὶ τοῦ βήματος—a passage to which Lutz fails to draw attention.

[1] See the scholiast, however, on Plat. Charm. 163 b: ἐ. τοῦ δεσμωτηρίου, ὡς Λυσίας, ἢ ἐ. πορνείου, ὡς Ἀττικοί.

64

B.

Examples of ἐπί in the Attic Inscriptions.

The following are the instances of ἐπί c. gen. and dat. in local sense in the Attic Inscriptions down to 300 B. C.:

ἐπί c. Dat.

Vol. I 1, 40 βωμῷ.
273, 14 Σουνίῳ.
273, 22 Παλλαδίῳ, also in l. 5.
321, 20 τοίχῳ, also in l. 43. = at.
322, 9 γονίᾳ ad angulum Boeckh.
322, 83 προστάσει ad porticum B.

Vol. I 322, 90 ἐπιστυλίοις in epistyliis B.
324 a I 44 κυμάτιον ... τὸ ἐπὶ (sic) τῷ ἐπιστυλίῳ. So 324 c II 12.
432 a, 32 Σιδείῳ ("is locus, ubi terrarum situs fuerit ignoramus," Kirchh.).
Vol. II 163, 19 βωμῷ (twice).

ἐπί c. Gen.

Vol. I 31, 17 A τῶν ἐπὶ Θρᾴκης. So 181, 3. 446, 46.
157, 6 κόρη χρυσῆ ἐπὶ στήλης. So 170, 11. 173, 6.
319, 19 κλίμακε) ἐφ' ὧν οἱ λίθοι ἐσεκομίζοντο.

Vol. I 322, 44 τοίχου ad parietem Boeckh. So lines 51, 67.
322, 86 κορῶν supra puellas B.
324 c I 18 τὸν ἄνδρα τὸν ἐπὶ τῆς βακτηρίας εἰστηκότα.
Vol. II 167, 63 τοίχου.

C.

Table showing the Local Use of ὑπό.

	Gen. = sub	= ὑπέκ	Total Gens.	Dative.	Total Dats.	Accus.	Total Accs.
Hom. and Hym.	28	17 (18)	133 (134)	109	212	70	72
Hesiod	12	2	32	14	25	2	2
Pindar	3	4	12	12	26	5	6
Aesch.	7	0	48	15	22	14	14
Soph.	10	0	60	10	10	5	6
Eurip.	12 (13)	5 (4)	135	41	45	29	30
Aristoph.	1 (?)	1 (?)	157	6	9	9	12
Herodot.	0	1 (?)	457	14	40	22	45
Thucyd.	0	0	366	4	13	6	43
Xenoph.	0	2	702	28	52	24	33
Orators	0	0	1294	8	63	See note.	26
Plato	[6	0	?	5	16	13	15]

In preparing this table I have relied in the case of Homer, Pindar, Aesch., Soph., Aristoph., Thucyd., the Orators, and Plato, upon the lexicons of Ebeling, Rumpel, Dindorf, Ellendt, Sobolewski (dissertation), Van Essen, Lutz, and Ast respectively. The last-named is of course incomplete, and I have bracketed the figures. For the other authors the count is my own. The following notes may be added as explanatory, or of interest:

The phrases ὑπὸ σκότον, -ου, -ῳ (ζόφον, σκιᾶς, αὐγάς, εὐδίαν) have been included in the list as local, the metaphor being a vivid one, if indeed they are to be reckoned as metaphors. But the phrases δαμῆναι (τεθνάναι, etc.) ὑπὸ χερσί (παλάμῃσι, etc.) τινος, or ὑπό τινι, have been excluded from the purely local list, as also ὑπὸ μάλης. This last phrase has certainly lost all literal significance, as shown by the word itself, which occurs only in the genitive and only in this phrase (μασχάλη being the literal word). These are almost certain marks of "adverbiale Erstarrung,"[1] rendered doubly certain here by the fact that the sense of *occulte* is necessary in some and admissible in all of the passages where it is found, viz. Aristoph. Lys. 985. Xen. Hell. II 3, 23. Lysias Frg. 54. Dem. 29, 12. Plat. Gorg. 469 *d*, Leg. VII 789 *c*. Sobolewski is inclined to admit this: "nescio an hic quoque (Lys. 985) haec significatio (*clanculum* vel *occulte*) praeferenda sit," but Lutz quotes the Lysias fragment as "das einzige *lokale* Beispiel für ὑπό c. gen. bei den attischen Rednern."

In the usage of the individual authors the following points may be noted:

Homer shows but two cases where ὑπό c. acc. may be taken as temporal, Π 202 ὑπὸ μηνιθμόν, X 102 νύχθ' ὕπο. The *sub imperio* sense of ὑπό c. dat., which is steady and frequent throughout, begins in Homer with nine instances, at the head of which may stand ὑπὸ σκήπτρῳ—the source perhaps of all the others.

Hesiod, according to Rzach's constitution of the text, shows ὑπό c. acc. only twice, one of these being ὑπὸ χθόνα Theog. 304, the other οὐρὰς δ' ὑπό, Op. 512.

Pindar uses ὑπό c. dat. seven times to express agent, against ὑπό c. gen. five times. His preference here therefore, as well as in the local use, should decide for the dat. in Ol. VI 40 λόχμαις ὑπὸ κυανέαις, altogether aside from the question of picturesqueness (as one item of which note the imperf. tense of ἔτικτε). Note also the difference between ὑπ' Αἴτνας Ol. XIII 111 and ἐπ' ὀφρύι Παρνασσίᾳ

[1] See Brugmann, *Griech. Gram.*, §175 (p. 200).

v. 106, *the latter in a careful enumeration*. Among the five local accusatives, ὑπὸ γᾶν once, ὑπὸ χθόνα twice. Like Hesiod, he has no temporal accus.

Aeschylus.—In the seven local genitives, three are χθονός, one γῆς. Again there appears no temporal accusative.

Sophocles.—In the ten instances of the local gen. two are χθονός, three γαίας (γᾶς, γῆς). Note the difference between ὑπὸ στέγης Ant. 1248, which means no more than *under cover, clam*, and τῇδ' ὑπὸ στέγῃ pathetically pointed out by Philoctetes, Phil. 286. Sophocles too avoids the temporal accusative.

Euripides, as might be expected, reverts to the epic ὑπό, signifying ὑπέκ, four times—or, if we follow Weil in Orest. 1457, five times. (Phoen. 792 being surely corrupt (see Paley), has been excluded.) But he follows Hesiod, Pindar, Aesch., Soph. in using no temporal ὑπό c. accusative.

Aristophanes Av. 1070 ὑπ' ἐμᾶς πτέρυγος has been admitted as local, with Sobolewski (*sub ala mea*), but is doubtful. Kock reads ἐπ'. So too Vesp. 206 ὑποδυόμενος ... ὑπὸ τῶν κεραμίδων has been taken to mean *desub tegulis* by Sobolewski. From the rarity of that meaning in post-Homeric Greek, this may be doubted, unless indeed there be hidden here a parody on Euripides. At last two temporal accusatives are met, Acharn. 139 ὑπ' αὐτὸν τὸν χρόνον, 1076 ὑπὸ τοὺς Χόας.

Herodotus 4, 8 is read by Stein and Krüger ὑπὸ τοῦ ἅρματος and translated as ὑπέκ. But Abicht, Baehr and others read ἀπό, and Van Herwerden casts out altogether. The nearest approach to a local gen. is ὑπὸ μαστίγων 7, 22 and 56. But this means *to the tune of the lash* just as in ὑπ' αὐλοῦ. Of the twenty-two local accusatives, ten are ὑπὸ γῆν; of the 14 temporal accusatives, nine are ὑπὸ νύκτα (ὑπὸ τὴν ... νύκτα, etc.)

Thucydides VII 75, 5 should not be read with Bekker (and Van Essen) ὑπὸ τοῖς ὅπλοις, but ἐπὶ τοῖς ὅπλοις with Pluygers. (See Classen.) In the forty-three instances of ὑπό c. accus., thirty-four are temporal—a remarkably high number as compared with

Xenophon, who in thirty-three accusatives has the temporal ὑπό c. acc. but twice. ὑπό c. gen. in the sense of ὑπέκ is said by Krüger to be seen in An. VI 2, 22 and 25.

The Orators.—According to Lutz, p. 179, "Der lokale Gebrauch (of ὑπό c. acc.) umfasst mehr als die Hälfte aller Beispiele, Antiphon und Andocides beschränken sich einzig und allein auf denselben."

Plato's usage is not fully reported by Ast., but is perhaps given complete in the rarer matters, as in the local gen. and dat. Of the six local instances of ὑπό c. gen., five are ὑπὸ γῆς.

The following dissertations have been consulted with more or less advantage in the preparation of this essay :

Sobolewski : De Praepositionum Usu Aristophaneo, 1890.
Lalin : De Praepositionum Usu apud Aeschylum, 1885.
Kuemmell : De Praepositionis ἐπί Usu Thucydideo, 1875.
Lutz : Die Praepositionen bei den attischen Rednern, 1887.
Krebs : Die Praepositionen bei Polybius, 1882.

Also La Roche's articles on the Homeric ἐπί and ὑπό in the *Zeitschrift für die Oesterr. Gymnas.*, vols. XII (1861), p. 352, and XXI (1870), p. 81, have been used. But my indebtedness to Professor Gildersleeve has been much greater than to any or all of these together.

www.ingramcontent.com/pod-product-compliance
Lightning Source LLC
Chambersburg PA
CBHW021519090426
42739CB00007B/688